Domestic Violence

Other Books in the Issues on Trial Series:

Domestic Violence

Kelly Barth, Book Editor

GREENHAVEN PRESS
A part of Gale, Cengage Learning

GALE
CENGAGE Learning·

Detroit • New York • San Francisco • New Haven, Conn • Waterville, Maine • London

Christine Nasso, *Publisher*
Elizabeth Des Chenes, *Managing Editor*

© 2009 Greenhaven Press, a part of Gale, Cengage Learning

For more information, contact:
Greenhaven Press
27500 Drake Rd.
Farmington Hills, MI 48331-3535
Or you can visit our Internet site at gale.cengage.com.

For product information and technology assistance, contact us at

Gale Customer Support, 1-800-877-4253
For permission to use material from this text or product, submit all requests online at
www.cengage.com/permissions

Further permissions questions can be emailed to permissionrequest@cengage.com

Articles in Greenhaven Press anthologies are often edited for length to meet page requirements. In addition, original titles of these works are changed to clearly present the main thesis and to explicitly indicate the author's opinion. Every effort is made to ensure that Greenhaven Press accurately reflects the original intent of the authors. Every effort has been made to trace the owners of copyrighted material.

Cover photograph © Mark Peterson/CORBIS.

LIBRARY OF CONGRESS CATALOGING-IN-PUBLICATION DATA

Domestic violence / Kelly Barth, book editor.
    p. cm. -- (Issues on trial)
    Includes bibliographical references and index.
    ISBN-13: 978-0-7377-4176-6 (hardcover)
    1. Family violence--United States--Case studies--Juvenile literature. I. Barth, Kelly.
    HV6626.2.D682 2009
    362.82'920973--dc22
                                        2008031447

Printed in the United States of America
1 2 3 4 5 6 7 12 11 10 09 08

Contents

Chapter 2: Police Are Not Obligated to Enforce Protection Orders

Chapter 3: Using Out-of-Court Statements as Testimony

Chapter 4: Prosecuting Domestic Abuse Cases Where No Marriage Exists

Foreword

The U.S. courts have long served as a battleground for the most highly charged and contentious issues of the time. Divisive matters are often brought into the legal system by activists who feel strongly for their cause and demand an official resolution. Indeed, subjects that give rise to intense emotions or involve closely held religious or moral beliefs lay at the heart of the most polemical court rulings in history. One such case was *Brown v. Board of Education* (1954), which ended racial segregation in schools. Prior to *Brown*, the courts had held that blacks could be forced to use separate facilities as long as these facilities were equal to that of whites.

For years many groups had opposed segregation based on religious, moral, and legal grounds. Educators produced heartfelt testimony that segregated schooling greatly disadvantaged black children. They noted that in comparison to whites, blacks received a substandard education in deplorable conditions. Religious leaders such as Martin Luther King Jr. preached that the harsh treatment of blacks was immoral and unjust. Many involved in civil rights law, such as Thurgood Marshall, called for equal protection of all people under the law, as their study of the Constitution had indicated that segregation was illegal and un-American. Whatever their motivation for ending the practice, and despite the threats they received from segregationists, these ardent activists remained unwavering in their cause.

Those fighting against the integration of schools were mainly white southerners who did not believe that whites and blacks should intermingle. Blacks were subordinate to whites, they maintained, and society had to resist any attempt to break down strict color lines. Some white southerners charged that segregated schooling was *not* hindering blacks' education. For example, Virginia attorney general J. Lindsay Almond asserted, "With the help and the sympathy and the love and respect of the white people of the South, the colored man has risen under that educational process to a place of eminence and respect throughout the nation. It has served him well." So when the Supreme Court ruled against the segregationists in *Brown*, the South responded with vociferous cries of protest. Even government leaders criticized the decision. The governor of Arkansas, Orval Faubus, stated that he would not "be a party to any attempt to force acceptance of change to which the people are so overwhelmingly opposed." Indeed, resistance to integration was so great that when black students arrived at the formerly all-white Central High School in Arkansas, federal troops had to be dispatched to quell a threatening mob of protesters.

Nevertheless, the *Brown* decision was enforced and the South integrated its schools. In this instance, the Court, while not settling the issue to everyone's satisfaction, functioned as an instrument of progress by forcing a major social change. Historian David Halberstam observes that the *Brown* ruling "deprived segregationist practices of their moral legitimacy. . . . It was therefore perhaps the single most important moment of the decade, the moment that separated the old order from the new and helped create the tumultuous era just arriving." Considered one of the most important victories for civil rights, *Brown* paved the way for challenges to racial segregation in many areas, including on public buses and in restaurants.

In examining *Brown*, it becomes apparent that the courts play an influential role—and face an arduous challenge—in shaping the debate over emotionally charged social issues. Judges must balance competing interests, keeping in mind the high stakes and intense emotions on both sides. As exemplified by *Brown*, judicial decisions often upset the status quo and initiate significant changes in society. Greenhaven Press's Issues on Trial series captures the controversy surrounding influential court rulings and explores the social ramifications of such decisions from varying perspectives. Each anthology highlights one social issue—such as the death penalty, students' rights, or wartime civil liberties. Each volume then focuses on key historical and contemporary court cases that helped mold the issue as we know it today. The books include a compendium of primary sources—court rulings, dissents, and immediate reactions to the rulings—as well as secondary sources from experts in the field, people involved in the cases, legal analysts, and other commentators opining on the implications and legacy of the chosen cases. An annotated table of contents, an in-depth introduction, and prefaces that overview each case all provide context as readers delve into the topic at hand. To help students fully probe the subject, each volume contains book and periodical bibliographies, a comprehensive index, and a list of organizations to contact. With these features, the Issues on Trial series offers a well-rounded perspective on the courts' role in framing society's thorniest, most impassioned debates.

Introduction

Anger and confusion have always gone hand in hand with domestic violence. The judicial system must deal with this anger and sift through this confusion to determine what really happened and ensure that all involved—from victim to police to abuser—are treated with respect. This is the balancing act today's courts have been called upon to perform.

Though certainly not the sole victims of domestic violence, women are by far its most likely targets. To protect themselves and their children, women often spend years lying to, cajoling with, and submitting to the men in their lives. Inevitably, this accommodation wears thin. When a man's abuse escalates, the woman may fear not only for her own safety, but also for her children's safety. In such situations, involving police can further provoke her abuser.

Vigilante Justice or Self-Defense?

Knowing this, some women resort to killing their abusers before the men can make good on their threats to severely injure or kill them. Historically, abused women have not fared well in the criminal justice system, especially when they have taken the law into their own hands. Men's and women's culturally proscribed roles have left abused women with few cards to play. Michael Dowd, an attorney and expert in the history of domestic violence, says "men were born and grew up with the certain constant that they were superior to women. Women in society were the nurturers, the care-givers, not the movers or shakers. It was the way things were meant to be. Many women grew up being taught—and accepted—the same beliefs. A woman's violence against a particular man in self-defense was seen as a threat to all men and the existing social order." Most women who have killed an abusive spouse have paid for their crimes with long prison sentences or even their lives.

When a woman kills an attacker she does not know, the courts are likely to classify her actions as self-defense, but until very recently, a woman who killed a man in response to domestic violence was viewed simply as a murderer. One of the most famous cases of a woman killing her abuser, *People v. Francine Hughes*, changed the court's thinking only slightly. The court ruled that despite being abused by her husband for more than a decade, Hughes must not have been in her right mind when she killed him. She was found not guilty by reason of temporary insanity.

Criticism of the decision varied widely. One camp maintained that justifying Hughes and other battered women's behavior, whether or not it was in response to violence, sanctioned vigilante justice. The courts, they maintained, must ensure that the life of every human, even that of an abuser, is protected from the murderous violence of another. Another camp comprised of feminist legal scholars countered that any sane person put in a similar situation would act as Hughes did.

To lend credibility to insanity pleas following cases like *People v. Hughes*, attorneys increasingly relied on a defense based on a sociological explanation for such behavior called the Battered Wife Syndrome (BWS). According to BWS, when a wife suffers physical and emotional isolation and abuse, she feels like a hostage, believing that her husband will kill her if she leaves. Because BWS sounds like a one-size-fits-all disorder of abused women, it has fallen out of favor with psychiatrists and feminists but is still used by defense attorneys seeking judicial leniency for their clients.

Protection from Law Enforcement Is Not a Right

Undoubtedly, law enforcement officials responding to often volatile domestic violence calls face no easy task. Many officers are understandably reluctant to take action in what many perceive as a private family matter. They must do their best to diffuse situations fraught with anger and confusion. Their failure to respond correctly or at all can result in serious injury or even death to the victims of domestic violence. Linda Knopf, director of a support group for domestic violence victims, maintains that police suffer from the same sexual biases as society at large. She says that "if the police aren't properly educated and trained, they'll believe in every case that the woman is crazy or violent, or in the worst case, that she's only harassing her partner to win a custody battle to get a larger financial settlement in a divorce case."

The judicial system has had to determine the extent to which law enforcement is legally responsible for providing proper intervention. The Supreme Court has ruled that even though a victim of domestic violence has an active protection order, she must rely on the police's discretion to enforce it, even though she and her children may be harmed or killed if the police do not do so. Victim advocates condemned the Court's response, saying it has left victims in a no-win situation: Women cannot depend on police protection, but they cannot legally take responsibility for their own protection either.

Must an Abused Woman Appear in Court?

Before domestic violence victims reach such a point of desperation, many rely on police and 911 operators for help. Accounts given to law enforcement have long been considered valuable information in a trial. Women fearful of facing an abusive partner have relied on the court's willingness to let these accounts represent them as evidence against their partner.

This all changed as the courts were confronted with claims that allowing such evidence violated the rights of the abuser. Attorneys for men accused of domestic violence maintained that if these women did not have to appear in court to confront their partners, the men's right to be confronted by their accuser, which is protected under the Sixth Amendment to the Constitution, would be violated. Ultimately, the Supreme Court decided that transcripts of calls occurring during abuse were admissible since they were not used to prove a crime had been committed but to report one occurring in the present. On the other hand, police interviews given after the violence had occurred were not admissible because they were an attempt to prove such an event had occurred.

Again, response to the Court's action was mixed. Some accused the Court of protecting the civil rights of the accused. Others felt the Court was allowing for the helpful cross-examination of a witness. Cross-examination is especially beneficial when reviewing an incident that is guaranteed to be emotionally charged and rife with confusion. However, critics said the Court's thinking might prevent prosecution of the crime of domestic violence altogether. Often the only witnesses to such crimes, abused women, are justifiably fearful of facing the men who have abused them. With this new precedent, abusers receive the lion's share of protection rather than their victims. If the information law enforcement collects from women cannot be used in court, then abusers could walk free.

The Unforeseen Consequences of Marriage Amendments

With the rise in state marriage amendments, the courts have faced a host of unforeseen challenges to domestic violence convictions. Originally designed to prevent homosexuals from marrying, marriage amendments have since been used in ways that have stripped domestic violence victims of legal protection. Courts have had to decide if a heterosexual who is not legally married according to a marriage amendment can still be convicted of domestic violence under state statutes. The amendments also challenge the idea that partners in a homosexual relationship can be protected under a domestic violence statute since they are not living in a legally recognized relationship.

Those who are against homosexual marriage fear that if law enforcement uses domestic violence statutes to convict men of domestic violence who are not living in a legal marriage, such convictions could be used to undermine state marriage amendments. Any state statute recognizing someone as a spouse who is simply living with someone, they say, must be rewritten.

The Balancing Act Continues

People caught in the throes of domestic violence remain at the mercy of the judicial system. While court decisions must affirm the humanity of victims, they must also protect the basic civil rights of abusers. Critics of the judicial system say that it is failing everyone touched by domestic violence. Statistics agree. The number of abused women continues to increase. Intimate partner assaults are rarely prosecuted as anything more than a misdemeanor. Though the BWS defense keeps some abuse victims who murder their intimate partners from going to jail, many are still serving time for defending themselves and their children against their abusers when law enforcement did not. The vast majority of abusers sentenced to batterer intervention programs in exchange for jail time continue to abuse after completing such programs. Evan Stark, a professor of urban health administration at the University of Medicine and Dentistry of New Jersey, laments the lack of judicial progress being made. He says, "having let domestic violence pass without much notice for centuries, it is hardly surprising that society hesitates before enforcing zero tolerance as a norm. Nor should we be shocked to find the same legal system that was unimpressed by partner violence only moments ago (historically speaking) resisting the mandate to harshly sanction this behavior or that piecemeal reforms have failed to dislodge long-running patterns of abuse."

CHAPTER 1

Murder as Self-Defense?

Case Overview

The People v. Francine Hughes (1977)

On March 8, 1977, Francine Hughes put her children and some belongings in the car, poured gasoline around the bed where her husband Mickey slept, and threw a lit match into the room. A Michigan jury had to determine if she could be charged with murder or found innocent by reason of temporary insanity caused by years of physical and emotional abuse. Her defense attorney, Ayron Greydanus, encouraged her to make such a plea because he believed a jury would never view Hughes' actions as self-defense, even if they understood the depth of her fear that her husband would soon kill her.

Like many women caught in a cycle of abuse, Hughes had difficulty leaving her husband, which might seem surprising. Throughout their marriage, Mickey Hughes had alternately abused Francine and then begged her forgiveness when she threatened to leave him permanently. Since she had left him once, the prosecuting attorney argued, why couldn't she have left him this final time? He argued that, rather than the impulsive act of a mentally unstable individual, the murder was the calculated, premeditated act of an entirely sane one. Upon cross-examination, however, even the psychiatrist whom the prosecution had called to convince the jury that Hughes had been sane at the time of the murder, agreed during Greydanus's cross-examination that she could not possibly have planned such a violent act. Without premeditation, the prosecution could not convince the jury that Hughes had been in her right mind at the time of the murder. They found her not guilty.

The *Hughes* case represented a turning point for battered women. She was the first woman found not guilty of murdering her abusive husband. The case garnered national attention, with Hughes appearing twice on the talk show *Donahue*.

A made-for-TV movie, *The Burning Bed*, starring Farrah Fawcett, dramatized her abusive marriage, the trial and her ultimate acquittal.

For a variety of reasons, the trial has continued to generate controversy. Some insisted that by allowing Hughes to murder her abusive husband and go free and unpunished, the court set a frightening legal precedent. In an entirely different camp, feminist legal scholars expressed disappointment over Greydanus's decision to encourage Hughes to plead temporary insanity. What sane person, they ask, faced with similar threats to her well-being, wouldn't have considered a similar action? These scholars argue that Greydanus should have called for a reexamination of the traditional legal understanding of self-defense. Until then, it had been applied to cases of confrontation between two strangers of equal strength and ability, not to a man and woman in a relationship where a great physical and culturally imposed power disparity likely existed.

The *Hughes* case and subsequent cases like it led to the formulation of something called the Battered Wife Syndrome (BWS) defense. Victims of BWS, sociologists assert, are so demoralized by abuse, they do not believe escape from an abusive husband is possible. Many believe killing their batterer is their only means of escape. Like many other mental conditions, BWS is difficult to firmly diagnose. Consequently, it remains a controversial legal defense.

> *"I do not think that her actions repre-*
> *sented premeditation and planning . . .*
> *She did not sit back and think, 'I'm go-*
> *ing to kill my husband now.'"*

Physical and Mental Abuse
Leads a Victim to Murder

Faith McNulty

After years of abuse, Francine Hughes put her children in her
car, poured gasoline around the bed where her husband slept,
and threw a lit match into the room. Journalist Faith McNulty's
book about Hughes' life, The Burning Bed, *includes the follow-*
ing account of the trial that would ultimately find Hughes inno-
cent of her husband's death by reason of temporary insanity.
Psychiatrists who offered testimony maintained that a sane per-
son could not have planned such a crime. The lack of premedita-
tion on Hughes' part would make her one of the first domestic
violence victims who killed her abuser to escape a murder charge.

Although it was mid-afternoon when Francine finished testifying, [her attorney Aryon] Greydanus decided to bring
on his next witness before the mood Francine had created
could slip away. He called Dr. Arnold Berkman, the clinical
psychologist who would explain Francine's act in terms of
temporary insanity. . . .

When Greydanus asked for his evaluation of Francine, Dr.
Berkman read from his report: "My examination revealed no
evidence of psychosis but did reveal defects in psychological

functioning and personality development which reflect significant psychopathology . . . characterized by deeply ingrained maladaptive patterns of behavior which have brought her tremendous pain. . . ."

"Mrs. Hughes has a strong need for approval, developed in response to her lifelong feelings of vulnerability and powerlessness. . . . She experiences little sense of competence, self-confidence, or autonomy, making it easy for her to be overwhelmed, tremendously threatened, and easily controlled by those whom she perceives as more powerful than herself."

Doctors Define Temporary Insanity

Dr. Berkman explained that Francine's strong need for approval, coupled with her belief that to be a "good wife" meant to be a slave of one's husband, and her well-founded fear of retribution if she angered [her husband] Mickey, caused Francine to suppress her own anger year after year, until the marriage became "a horror show," in which she was almost literally imprisoned. Berkman testified that her terror of Mickey's revenge if she tried to leave him was vividly real, and was constantly reinforced by his beating her if she dared even to visit a friend or her family. "She believed he would find her and kill her wherever she went. She was hopelessly trapped both by her own profound psychological conflicts and by her realistic fear of her husband."

Berkman described how much it had meant to Francine to go to school. By forcing her to burn her books, Mickey "was forcing her to kill that part of herself which was on the threshold of independence . . . to symbolically kill herself and all that she had invested and suffered in trying to be a person."

When Francine killed Mickey, Berkman said, "she was overwhelmed by the massive onslaughts of her most primitive emotions. Emotions she had suppressed for so many years overwhelmed her. . . . She experienced a breakdown of her psychological processes so that she was no longer able to utilize judgment . . . no longer able to control her impulses . . . unable to prevent herself from acting in the way she did.

"Anger is an emotion which creates considerable distress for her, and since anger runs counter to her quest for approval, she is unable to express anger directly. In terms of her life, particularly her marriage, it is appropriate she should be enraged. It is part of her psychological sickness that she could not get angry, feel angry, react with anger to a situation that was so deeply humiliating, dehumanizing, and physically cruel. . . ."

When Berkman finished reading his report, Greydanus asked, "Dr Berkman, is Francine a person who could plan a murder?"

"No."

"Why do you say that?"

"The ability to plan a murder would require an ability to think ahead, wait, plan for the proper time. Francine is not good at doing those things. Her style is to behave very impulsively, sometimes with very poor judgment. Also, it is not in her character to plan something with such a degree of violence. Something like this would be abhorrent to her if she thought about it in advance or tried to plan it."

It was time to ask Berkman for the diagnosis that could win Francine's freedom.

"Dr. Berkman, at the time Francine committed this act was she mentally ill?"

"Yes, she was."

"Was she mentally ill to the extent that she could not conform to the law, or control her behavior? Was she operating under an irresistible impulse?"

"Yes, she was."

"And at the time you examined her subsequently she was *not* mentally ill?"

"That is correct."

Greydanus could only hope he had sufficiently underlined the distinction between temporary insanity and mental illness. He thanked Berkman and the session ended. The jury would have all night to mull over Berkman's words.

When court convened the following morning, the seventh day of Francine's trial. [Prosecuting attorney] Palus questioned Dr. Berkman in an effort to construe his diagnosis in a way that would, under Michigan law, make Francine criminally responsible for murder.

"Dr. Berkman, would you tell us what your diagnosis of Francine Hughes was?"

"Borderline syndrome with hysterical and narcissistic features."

"Isn't it true that many people with borderline syndrome can tell the difference between right and wrong? Can understand the nature of their acts?"

"Yes. That's true. However, you are leaving out a crucial point. People with borderline syndrome, when a certain kind of stress impinges on them . . . at that particular time those people can fall apart. It's what we call psychological decompensation. It's very typical of these people."

"Now, Doctor, isn't it a fact that lots of people who are not mentally ill do things that are wrong and that they know are wrong?"

"Yes, that's true."

"And lots of people who are mentally ill do things that they know are wrong when they do them?"

"True."

"The fact that the defendant may have done some wrong things doesn't prove that she didn't know they were wrong, does it?"

"No. It doesn't prove that; it doesn't show that she necessarily did or didn't know that they were wrong."

"All right. In your opinion when did Francine Hughes recover from borderline syndrome?"

"She has not as yet recovered from it."

"So, borderline syndrome is not a psychosis; is that correct, Doctor?"

"My diagnosis is not a diagnosis of what she was like during those moments on March 9, 1977. It is a diagnosis of her entire personality." . . .

As his final witness Greydanus called Dr. Anne Seiden to the stand. Dr. Seiden, a small woman in her early forties, gave the court her extensive credentials, including her current position as staff psychiatrist at Michael Reese Hospital in Chicago. In a firm, quiet voice she described Francine's moment of "decompensation" in much the same terms Dr. Berkman had used.

"On the basis of that, Dr. Seiden," Greydanus asked, "did you make any findings concerning Francine's criminal responsibility at the time she committed this crime?"

"Yes," Dr. Seiden said. "I believe she was mentally ill at that time. She was unable to form a criminal intent because she lacked the capacity to appreciate the difference between right and wrong."

"Dr. Seiden, could she have stopped herself from doing what she did?"

"I don't believe she could have. She was in a state of ego fragmentation."

"What do you mean by ego fragmentation?"

"By that I mean that the part of the personality which ordinarily keeps one's understanding and impulses under control was not functioning. She was, in other words, acutely psychotic."

"Is that what we laymen call insane?"

"That's right," Dr. Sieden replied. . . .

The trial would close with the testimony of Dr. Blunt, the expert in legal psychiatry engaged by the prosecution to refute Berkman and Seiden. The brutalities of the life that Francine had endured with Mickey had been as clear to Blunt as to Seiden and Berkman, and in his written pretrial report Blunt had cited very similar details.

Where Blunt differed with Seiden and Berkman was whether, at the moment she poured the gasoline and lit it, Francine was legally insane. Michigan law defines insanity as "a substantial disorder of thought or mood which significantly impairs judgment, behavior, capacity to recognize reality, or ability to cope with ordinary demands of life." At the conclusion of his report, Dr. Blunt wrote: "In my opinion, Mrs. Hughes shows no evidence of any disorder that would render her mentally ill in accordance with MCL 330.1400a [the statute defining mental illness], either at the time of the incident or at the present time." . . .

"Dr. Blunt," Greydanus began. "How long did you examine Francine Hughes?"

"For one hour and forty minutes."

"And you have testified that she gave you her entire history, all the background, an explanation of what her character is like, and her motivations?"

"Yes. I think she did."

"Do you feel you acquired all the information you needed in that hour and forty minutes?"

"Yes, I did." Dr. Blunt bridled. "Or I would have taken longer."

Wasn't there a possibility, Greydanus insisted, that deeper examination might have turned up the "previous episodes" that Blunt had said would be needed to convince him that Francine was subject to borderline syndrome?

"Yes," Blunt acknowledged after considerable hairsplitting. "You could always miss something." But he continued to maintain that Francine had not "decompensated" into an abnormal state of mind. He considered the voice she had heard urging her to "Do it! Do it!" to be evidence of a conflict of feeling rather than a hallucination.

Greydanus turned to Blunt's report on Francine.

"Doctor, on page six you indicate that her pent-up hostilities reached a stage where she 'chose' a course that would 'end the situation forever.' My question is, how do you know she could make a choice at that time?"

"By my interview with her. By talking with her about it."

"Well, Francine is the one who told you she heard voices; isn't that correct?"

"She told me she heard a voice saying, 'Do it! Do it! Do it!'"

"And you just sort of concluded that that wasn't the case; that she actually didn't hear those voices?"

"I did not feel it was an attempt on her part to feign hallucination. I felt it was her way of explaining how she felt at the time—of expressing her strong conflicting impulses."

"But despite your statement that you didn't feel she would make it up, or feign it, you are making the end judgment that she didn't really hear those voices?"

"I am making a judgment based on my clinical experience and training."

At least the doctor had admitted that Francine hadn't feigned hearing a voice. Now Greydanus asked if Dr. Blunt hadn't contradicted himself when he said that Francine "chose" a course, but at the same moment her "pent-up hostilities broke forth."

"No, I don't think so. I think that some things happened that night that were particularly devastating to her, and this brought a level of hostility which she was no longer able to keep under wraps."

"Did Francine have an immense fear of her ex-husband?"

"Yes. She did."

"And isn't it true that there is an element of self-defense in what she did?"

"Yes. Yes. She was defending herself in a sense. Not directly, because he was certainly not attacking her at that instant, but he had told her he would always follow her if she tried to get away—find her and harm her. I think she believed that was a real possibility; that wasn't an idle threat on his part."

Dr. Blunt had made a concession of great value to Francine's defense. Now Greydanus decided to play his big card.

"Let me ask you, Doctor, in studying Francine's character and everything that happened that night, in your opinion did her actions that night indicate premeditation and planning?"

"In my opinion," Blunt replied, "I do not think that her actions represented premeditation and planning. In other words, she did not sit back and think, 'I'm going to kill my husband now!' It was an impulsive thing that happened."

Greydanus felt a rush of triumph as he repeated the doctor's words, nailing them down.

"It was an *impulsive* thing? There was no planning? *No premeditation?*"

"I see no evidence of that."

"Thank you very much, Doctor," Greydanus said with sincerity, and sat down.

"Further questions, Mr. Palus?" Judge [Ray] Hotchkiss inquired.

"No redirect. Thank you, Your Honor," Palus replied, and the testimony in the case of *The People versus Francine Hughes* was at an end.

"The legal profession bears responsibility for having discouraged domestic assault prosecutions, but the profession is not to blame for the unwise expansion of homicide defenses."

Wife Abuse Does Not Justify Homicide

Marilyn Mitchell

In 1977, housewife Francine Hughes was acquitted of charges of first-degree murder for setting her sleeping husband on fire in his bed. A jury found her not guilty by reason of temporary insanity. In the following piece written shortly after the verdict, feminist social critic Marilyn Mitchell makes clear that, though she sympathizes with women in Hughes' predicament, to exempt them from responsibility for murder sets a dangerous legal precedent. Turning a blind eye to these women's actions while convicting men of similar crimes also furthers sexual discrimination, the very thing that Hughes' feminist supporters were trying to abolish.

In the fall of 1977, the media reported the cases of several women who claimed that prior physical abuse led to the killing of their husbands. The first trial to gain national publicity involved Francine Hughes, who was charged with first degree murder in the March 9, 1977, death of her husband James [Mickey]. Mrs. Hughes, mother of four, had been subjected to abuse throughout her thirteen-year marriage. Claim-

Marilyn Mitchell, "Does Wife Abuse Justify Homicide?" *Wayne Law Review*, vol. 24, 1978, pp. 1705–1731. Copyright © 1978 Wayne State University Law School. Reproduced by permission.

ing that she was desperate and could not receive help from relatives or the prosecutor's office, Mrs. Hughes poured gasoline under the bed of her sleeping husband and set it afire. He died of smoke inhalation. Mrs. Hughes voluntarily reported the killing to police and was defended by a court-appointed attorney who did not think the jury would credit a plea of self-defense and so defended on grounds of insanity. On November 3, 1977, the jury found Mrs. Hughes not guilty by reason of insanity. Two weeks later, Mrs. Hughes was found sane and released after a one-hour interview at the state forensic center in Ypsilanti, Michigan.

On November 29, 1977, a Marquette County Circuit Judge acquitted another Michigan woman of second degree murder charges in the February 12, 1977, shooting death of her husband of twenty-four years. The decedent [deceased person] was unarmed at the time of his death. Mrs. Sharon McNerney, mother of three, pleaded self- defense based on her belief that her husband would follow through on his threat to kill her. She testified she had been beaten an average of once a month during the marriage and that her husband had been jailed briefly eighteen months before his death for shooting at her. The judge found Mrs. McNerney's testimony persuasive and accepted her plea of self-defense.

In early December, 1977, a Wallace, Idaho, woman pled self-defense to charges of murdering her husband. June Chandler, mother of six, killed her husband September 10, 1977, with an automatic rifle after he beat and threatened to kill her. She testified that throughout the marriage, he had beaten and sexually abused her when he was intoxicated. He had been drinking the night of his death. She testified that she used the automatic weapon rather than any of the other guns in the house because, "I knew all you had to do was keep pulling the trigger. You didn't have to stop and reload." The jury acquitted Mrs. Chandler.

Also in early December, 1977, Wanda Carr of Redding, California, pled not guilty by reason of insanity in the shooting death of her husband of twenty-two years. Mrs. Carr had placed a loaded gun in the bedroom closet, and on the night of July 7, 1977, took the weapon, pointed it at her husband, woke him and asked that they talk. When he moved toward her, she killed him. The deputy district attorney who tried the case, voluntarily reduced the charge from murder to manslaughter and said, after the verdict, that he had not cared whether he won or lost. Shasta County Superior Court Judge Richard Abbe, who acquitted the defendant, reportedly said, "I don't think she had a viable alternative. This was a classic case in the sense of a long period of abuse and harassment. . . . It was serious protracted mental and physical abuse."

An Illinois woman, Mrs. Patricia Evans, plead guilty to the shooting death of her husband in April, 1976, and was sentenced to serve two to six years. Her attorney said he did not argue the case because "I thought at the time it would have been very difficult to prove self-defense. She had to load the pistol, follow him down three flights of stairs and shoot him." The killing followed a brutal beating where the decedent pistol whipped the defendant. Mrs. Evans, mother of four children, had filed for divorce and had taken her husband to a mental health center for treatment some time prior to the killing. She had also complained to the police of assaults for the preceding five years. On December 6, 1977, Governor James R. Thompson commuted Mrs. Evans' sentence. A spokesman for the governor said the sentence was reduced because of "extenuating circumstances and because of the children."

In contrast to Mrs. Evans who did not contest the charges, Jennifer Patri of Waupaca, Wisconsin, aided by feminists and defense funds, decided to fight. On March 24, 1977, Mrs. Patri shot and killed her husband of thirteen years, following an argument over custody of two children. A divorce was pending. Following the shooting, the accused cleaned up the blood, wrapped the body in plastic, removed it to the farm's smoke-house, and set the building on fire. Firemen found the body and Mrs. Patri was charged with murder in the first degree. She later claimed that she had killed in self-defense when her husband threatened her with a knife. The prosecutor argued against self-defense since the decedent had been shot in the back, and claimed the fire was set to destroy evidence. A jury subsequently convicted Mrs. Patri on the lesser charge of voluntary manslaughter; she was sentenced in February, 1978, to ten years at hard labor. Both verdict and sentence are being appealed [Patri was sent to a mental hospital in Wisconsin, transferred to prison and paroled in 1980].

A case that received widespread media attention in the late fall of 1977 was that of Roxanne Gay, who stabbed her pro-football player husband to death as he slept. Mrs. Gay originally claimed self-defense by reason of an alleged four year period of physical abuse, and feminist groups on the East Coast rallied to her defense. By December, 1977, it was reported that her attorneys were considering an insanity defense as well as self-defense by reason of abuse. Early in 1978, Mrs. Gay's retained attorneys withdrew from the case in favor of Ian Wachstein of the Camden, New Jersey Public Defender's Office. According to Wachstein, there was not "one scintilla of evidence to support wife abuse" even though Mrs. Gay did file one abuse complaint with police which was later withdrawn. Police records revealed that Mrs. Gay's calls involved non-abuse complaints, such as auto theft. Furthermore, hospital records refuted Mrs. Gay's original contentions that she had been treated for injuries inflicted by her husband. In February, 1978, at a pre-trial hearing, Mrs. Gay was found to have been insane at the time of the killing and was committed to the Trenton State Psychiatric Hospital. The criminal charges against her were dismissed, and she was committed to the institution until she is found not to be a danger to herself or others.

To date, no verdict of acquittal has been based expressly on wife abuse as a defense to homicide. The defendants have either claimed insanity or self-defense based on a specific incident. The cases reveal, however, that both traditional defenses have been stretched beyond their common law and statutory definitions to allow acquittals or conviction on a lesser charge. We can expect to see more women allege wife abuse as a catalyst for killing because of these defendants' successes. . . .

Lawyers Must Present the Best Defense

The legal profession bears responsibility for having discouraged domestic assault prosecutions, but the profession is not to blame for the unwise expansion of homicide defenses that has followed from society's failure to deal with abuse. Once a homicide prosecution is brought, the defense attorney has the duty to "represent his client zealously within the bounds of the law." He must present the best defense available. Thus, if the lawyer has a choice between pleading self-defense for a possible acquittal and provocation which would only mitigate the punishment, he should plead the former and let the fact-finder decide the issue. Similarly, the prosecutor as the state's advocate will, if the facts allow, argue a case of murder in the first degree to attain the maximum penalty, knowing that other degrees of homicide are lesser included offenses. Because provocation is a defense, though only one of mitigation, it will not be urged by the state even if the facts point to provocation.

Thus, when juries and judges are confronted with a sympathetic defendant on the one hand and, on the other, a choice between finding her guilty of murder or acquitting her by expanding legal defenses, they may be less objective than the law theoretically requires. The cases discussed illustrate this phenomenon.

Wife abuse is a problem society cannot afford to ignore. Primarily, every person has the right not to be beaten and to have that right enforced by the police and the courts. Secondarily, a pattern of abuse, unacknowledged and untreated, leads, in a number of cases, to homicide. Tragically, family-related homicides are among the few we can predict, yet we are only beginning to comprehend the magnitude of domestic violence and propose methods for dealing with it. Once the homicide occurs, the state steps in to enforce society's prohibition of a killing that might have been prevented had society involved itself with the victim earlier.

Unfortunately, we have "discovered" the wife abuse problem as a result of recent trials of abused wives who killed their husbands. Dispositions of these cases reveal another evil that society as a whole may not yet recognize but which can have serious ramifications for our criminal justice system. When the facts of the cases are compared with legal defenses to homicide, it is obvious that definitions of justifiable homicide and provocation were broadened to accommodate these defendants.

None of the defendants responded with deadly force while they were in imminent danger, and the two women found insane for purposes of evading criminal responsibility were not subsequently adjudged insane for purposes of civil commitment. Of the women tried for homicide, two initiated actions on sleeping husbands. Two other women shot unarmed husbands who had threatened their lives. A fifth woman loaded a gun and pursued her husband down three flights of stairs to kill him. Another woman shot her husband in the back and concealed his body. One woman was legally divorced, although living with her ex-husband at the time of the killing, and divorce was pending for two others. There is no evidence that any of the women could not have escaped from their husbands at the time of the killing.

An Unjust Validation of Violence

When homicide defenses are stretched beyond their legal limits in abused wife murder cases, society essentially carves out an exception to general principles and sanctions homicide for a particular class of persons. This is the other side of the coin from the special treatment society, through its laws and law enforcement, affords to husbands who abuse their wives. In effect, society does not enforce assault law against men who beat their wives but punishes men who beat their neighbors. Similarly, abused wives who retaliate with deadly force against an abusive husband appear to be getting favored treatment from judges and juries in derogation of the law.

To establish a "battered wife" defense comparable to self-defense, as some propose, would be to exempt a class of citizens from the penalties imposed by law for homicide. This would not only validate a kind of vigilante justice the law is supposed to preclude, but would also establish a virtual sex discrimination classification such as society is now trying, by such proposals as the Equal Rights Amendment, to eliminate.

Failure to apply and enforce the law evenhandedly against all offenders is to condone violence and to foster personal, violent solutions to situations which, though occurring within the home, are nonetheless a legitimate concern of society as a whole.

> "What you sense is the making of a new code, or the adoption, maybe, of the worst of the old male-dominated one."

The Insanity Plea of an Abused Wife Cannot Withstand Scrutiny

Richard Cohen

Because she says she believed her life was in danger, Francine Hughes set her abusive husband's bed on fire while he slept. A jury found her not guilty of murder by reason of temporary insanity. Washington Post *writer Richard Cohen says, in the following editorial, that he sees no difference between vigilante justice carried out by men and Hughes' act of what feminists have called "heroism." Why could she not, Cohen asks, simply have left the dangerous marriage she found herself in? He asserts that instead, she took the law into her own hands and should have been held responsible for doing so.*

By way of getting around to the woman in Michigan who killed the man who was beating her, I'd like to start with something called "tings"—as in the expression, "Here's the ting, kid." Tings were always being explained to you in places like high school locker rooms or street corners and one of the tings you had to know was that there was justice and then there was justice. The first kind is what you learned in school and the second is what you learned in life. It was the second one that allowed you to hit women. That, as they said, was the ting.

Richard Cohen, "Vigilante Justice Back in Women's Movement," *The Washington Post,* December 4, 1977, pp. B1–B3. Reproduced by permission.

In fact, there were times when you almost had to hit women. Of course, there were all kinds of borderline situations that were discussed for hours, but there were other times when everyone would agree that a good shot in the mouth was in order, everyone nodding and saying yeah, there being no question of what had to be done. An example of that, for instance, being any example of when a woman had cheated on a man, cheating being broadly defined as anything that made the man lose face.

After a while, you sort of caught on to the fact that there was a whole body of pseudolaw on the subject of male-female relations and that sometimes this law took precedence over the other law. I mean, you were told that you could kill another man for offenses that had to do with your woman and you could beat her and you could get away with all this because the law would either look the other way or would, in its wisdom, support you. These were basic rules, something akin to self-defense or the notion that you could kill someone for trespassing on your property, especially after you had put up a piece of paper saying "Posted."

Vigilante Justice

Anyway, this was all part of that business that may be called something like frontier justice or vigilante justice or whatever. But it meant in some neighborhoods that you could pound someone to a tender state if they happened to brush against you on the street and you had to fight if you happened to get what is known as a dirty look—"what you looking at, man?" It all was explained with the wonderful sentence—"A man's got to do what a man's got to do." A good deal of the time, what men had to do involved women and most of the time these women were a good deal weaker and smaller, a fact that mattered not one whit and explains why some battered women are still asked what they did to provoke their husbands.

Now, we come to Francine Hughes who has become . . . a "symbol" and who has been hailed by some elements of the women's movement as a heroine of some kind. What Hughes did, not to put too fine a point on it, was douse her former husband's bed with gasoline and toss a match into it as he slept. Those are the basic facts, but there are mitigating circumstances aplenty and it is those that lend the case to the cause of feminism.

The facts are worth spelling out. For something like thirteen years, Mrs. Hughes endured a marriage in which she was beaten, throttled and, from time to time, chased around the house by her knife-wielding husband. Four children were born of this union, but back in 1971, Mrs. Hughes decided she had had enough. She divorced her husband, moving back only after he became injured in a car accident. He never changed his ways, though, and on the day he died he not only beat his former wife, but somehow forced her to burn the books she had bought for a course she was taking at a local business college.

How Is Hughes' Behavior Different Than Her Husband's?

There is a lot to the Hughes case that makes it less than the perfect case, even for militant feminists. First of all, the jury failed to see things the same way as some of Mrs. Hughes' supporters and did not acquit on the basis of self-defense, but on grounds of temporary insanity. Mrs. Hughes stands ready to make speeches anyway, her topic . . . being wife abuse. She might explain, while she's at it, why she moved back in with a man who had been brutalizing her for thirteen years and why she stuck around for such punishment. This is often the question when it comes to wife-beating, but in this case Hughes had already proved that she had a place to go and could live on her own.

No matter. Militant feminists have seized upon her case as something of a precedent, establishing right off that a woman has the right to defend herself from the attacks of a brutal husband, even kill him if need be. The fact that she killed him after thirteen years of this sort of thing apparently means nothing and the fact that she killed him as he slept also apparently means nothing. In fact, the fact that she did to him what he had never done to her—namely, take his life—seems to matter not at all. What matters is something else and while it is hard to figure out what to call it, you can call it a new kind of justice.

What you sense is the making of a new code, or the adoption, maybe, of the worst of the old, male-dominated one— the notion that for certain kinds of behavior a rough, vigilante justice is in order. It was that notion that troubled me when feminists argued that Inez Garcia [victim of domestic violence] was justified in shooting the man who had earlier raped her and it is that notion that troubles me in the Hughes case. It is not that neither woman had been wronged, it is only that they took it upon themselves to administer justice and they did not make the punishment fit the crime. They worked according to their own code and they were defended and excused by some according to this special code. It is as if they said. "A woman's got to do what a woman's got to do,"— which, give or take a word or two, is exactly what you learned years ago in locker rooms and street corners.

Back then it was a ting and not a movement.

> *"Battered women who kill their abusive partners behave as would any reasonable, sane person in their situation."*

A Sane Woman Protects Herself

Sarah Geraghty

Francine Hughes was charged with first degree murder for setting fire to the bed where her abusive husband slept. Though throughout her thirteen-year marriage she had sought help from the police and others, she received none. Her defense attorney had her plead temporary insanity because he feared she would not win her case based on a self-defense plea. A jury found her not guilty. Sarah Geraghty, author of the Michigan Women's Justice and Clemency Project's Clemency Manual *maintains that Hughes was entirely justified in murdering her husband as he represented an imminent danger to her. In the following selection from the manual, she argues that now an attorney would have far less difficulty than Hughes' attorney feared he would have convincing a jury that, in killing her husband, she was an entirely sane woman acting in her own self-defense.*

Before 1980, lawyers defending battered women who killed their spouses typically employed an excuse theory of defense. In 1977, a twenty-nine-year old housewife, Francine Hughes, was charged with first degree murder for killing her abusive husband. After enduring thirteen years of vicious beatings, death threats, intimidation, and humiliation, Ms.

Sarah Geraghty, *The Clemency Manual*, Introduction and Chapter IV, *Clemency for Battered Women in Michigan: A Manual for Attorneys, Law Students and Social Workers*, 1998. www.umich.edu. Reproduced by permission.

Hughes set fire to the bed in which her husband was sleeping. For years before the murder, Ms. Hughes tried to escape from her husband without success. She actively sought help from lawyers, judges, social service agencies, and the police, all to no avail. Had she not killed her husband, it seems probable that she would have died at his hands.

Ms. Hughes' defense counsel believed that a self-defense claim would be legally infirm because self-defense is defined as occurring in the presence of imminent [close and likely] danger. Ms. Hughes fought back at a moment when her husband was sleeping. At the time, Ms. Hughes' lawyer could not find a single precedent for an argument for self-defense in a case in which a woman killed her abuser in a non-confrontational situation.

Instead of relying on a self-defense claim, Ms. Hughes utilized an excuse defense—she claimed she had been temporarily insane when she killed her husband. An expert testified that she was "overwhelmed by the massive onslaughts of her most primitive emotions." In this case, temporary insanity was a successful defense. Ms. Hughes was found "not guilty."

Although the temporary insanity defense produced a just result in the Hughes case, it has lost favor for several reasons. First, temporary insanity is a perilous defense. A defendant acquitted because of temporary insanity goes free. But a defendant found "guilty but mentally ill" faces the same term in prison as a sane person.

A second flaw in the excuse defense is that it presumes that a battered woman suffers from a mental defect. Recent psychological and scholarly literature argues that, in fact, battered women who kill their abusive partners behave as would any reasonable, sane person in their situation.

Battered Women Who Kill Are Not Insane

Studies on (1) similarities between the Stockholm syndrome and the BWS [Battered Wife Syndrome] and (2) the phenomenon of "separation assault" have led to widespread rejection of the belief that battered women suffer from mental defect.

1. Similarities between the BWS and Stockholm Syndrome

Studies of similarities between the BWS and the Stockholm Syndrome support a feminist analysis of the BWS. The Stockholm Syndrome is a psychological theory which attempts to explain why a hostage bonds with her captor. Four conditions give rise to the development of the Stockholm Syndrome:

a. A captor threatens to kill a person, and is perceived as having the ability to do so.

b. The person cannot escape, so her life depends on the captor.

c. The person is isolated from outsiders.

d. The captor is perceived as showing some degree of kindness to the person.

The Stockholm Syndrome describes a group of behaviors which develop in response to a threat to survival posed by a captor. Hostages develop survival rather than escape skills because they see opportunities to escape as too dangerous to pursue. Because escape seems impossible, hostages respond to their situation by becoming highly attuned to the pleasures and displeasure of the captor. They cope with a continuous and immediate threat of death by adopting their captor's world view and assuming submissive postures.

Other behaviors attributable to the Stockholm Syndrome include:

• Victim denies anger at abuser and focuses on abuser's good qualities.

• Victim's "fight or flight" reactions are inhibited.

• Victim fears interference by authorities.

- Victim feels overwhelmingly grateful to the abuser for having spared her life.

- Victim fears that even though captor is jailed, he will return to capture her again.

Research on the Stockholm Syndrome suggests that the behaviors characteristic of battered women are not pathological or masochistic, but are what we would expect from an individual in a life threatening captor/captive situation. . . . Lower income women who continue to live with partners because they have no financial resources reported more partner bonding. In other words, women who are realistically the most unable to escape rationally perceive the impossibility of their situation and reasonably respond to it in the only way possible: by nurturing an emotional bond with the batterer. . . . Women who separated from partners but returned because their partner located them, or because he threatened to kill them, showed more partner bonding. Thus, the degree of "traumatic bonding" is rationally related to the degree to which a woman feels her life is in danger.

Despite the fact that battered women and hostages exhibit shared psychological responses to a similar experience, popular opinion condemns battered women who bond to their partners as masochistic, while sympathizing with hostages who bond to their captors. The media treats hostage situations as high drama, while a battered woman's plight is considered a private family affair. Outsiders are more likely to negotiate and win the release of hostages. Outsiders are often reluctant to involve themselves when a battered woman asks for help.

2. Separation Assault

Traumatic bonding may not be the only reason that a battered woman is reluctant to leave her abuser. She may have a perfectly reasonable belief that if she leaves, he will track her down and harm her or kill her. Law enforcement experts agree that leaving an abuser greatly increases the danger a woman faces. According to the Bureau of Justice Statistics, in 1994, women separated from their husbands had a violent victimization rate of 128 per 1,000.

Orders of protection and pressing criminal charges are not always sufficient to protect a battered woman when her batterer, recognizing his loss of power and control, comes after her. As is clear from the following incidents, some batterers will go to any length to hurt their former partners:

- Patricia Kastle, an Olympic skier, was shot by her former husband notwithstanding a protection order forbidding him from coming near her.

- For eight years, Lisa Bianco, of Indiana, feared the day her husband would be released from prison. When prison officials granted her husband an eight-hour pass, he drove directly to her home, broke in, and beat her to death with the butt of a shotgun.

- Shirley Lowery, a grandmother of eleven, was in the hallway of the courthouse where she had gone to get an order of protection when her former boyfriend stabbed her nineteen times with a butcher knife....

Recognition of the prevalence of separation assault supports the fact that a battered woman acting in self-defense is acting according to a rational perception of danger. Given the modern view that battered women who kill their spouses are not insane, but rather acting rationally in an effort to defend themselves, the excuse theory of defense is employed less often than it used to be.

"Learned Helplessness"

At first glance, the theory that battered women experience traumatic bonding would seem inconsistent when applied to a battered woman who killed. Some critics of using the BWS argue that there is an "inherent inconsistency of describing the battered woman's unhealthy mental state to show the reasonableness of her belief of imminent danger." In her article arguing against admissibility of expert testimony on the BWS, Mira Mihajlovich states that a battered woman's "learned helplessness" necessarily blurs her ability to form rational beliefs about when she is in imminent danger. Statutory and case law have also misconstrued the BWS as evidence in support of an excuse defense. For example, Missouri law has procedurally equated the BWS with an insanity plea by providing that a defendant who seeks to introduce evidence on the BWS must submit to an exam by a court appointed psychologist or psychiatrist. In addition, appellate opinions have characterized battered women as psychologically disturbed.

"Learned helplessness" is misinterpreted when it is defined as a mental defect or character flaw. The whole point of learned helplessness as a psychological theory is to remove the stigma of mental defect from the battered woman by emphasizing that the behaviors associated with it developed as an adaptive survival mechanism in response to abuse.

Angela Browne, author of *Assault and Homicide at Home: When Battered Women Kill*, explains that there is no inconsistency between learned helplessness and a battered woman who kills—that a battered woman ceases to practice the survival skills characterized by the Stockholm Syndrome when she endures an act of violence which is significantly above the normal range of violence she has previously experienced. A woman who kills her batterer often does so only when she thinks it is impossible to survive the next episode of abuse, or when the batterer escalates or threatens escalation of violence towards a child. Thus, the theory that battered women, like hostages, may experience traumatic bonding is consistent with the fact that some battered women ultimately kill their abusers in defense of their lives.

The Justification Defense

Today, a lawyer defending a woman in Francine Hughes' position would probably employ a justification defense. There is a common myth that most battered women kill while their husbands are asleep, or during a lull in the violence. Actually, about 70 percent of battered women who kill their batterers do so during a confrontation with the batterer. Thus, the trend toward a justification theory of defense is an appropriate one.

Use of a justification defense is still not without its problems, however. Legal scholars engage in hot debate over whether existing definitions of self-defense can accommodate battered women who kill their spouses.

In determining whether a defendant acted in self-defense, a trier of facts considers issues such as: (1) whether the defendant reasonably feared that she needed to use force to defend herself; (2) whether the threat to the defendant was imminent; (3) whether the defendant met the threat with excessive force; and (4) whether the defendant had a duty to retreat.

Some critics charge that battered women, like Francine Hughes, who killed their abusive partners in a non-confrontational situation cannot get a fair trial under existing definitions of self-defense. For example, Cynthia Gillespie, author of *Justifiable Homicide*, asserts that because self-defense jurisprudence requires a threat to be imminent, a woman who kills her batterer while he is sleeping is prevented from utilizing the defense. Specifically, Gillespie argues that under self-defense law strictly applied, a woman is not allowed to fight back with a weapon until her batterer actually beats her severely enough to make it clear that death or great bodily harm is imminent. Of course, by that time, she would be rendered helpless.

Critics of self-defense laws as they apply to battered women who kill also contend that traditional principles of self-defense jurisprudence are based on two men of equal strength who have never met, and that traditional principles do not consider the problems posed by combatants of vastly different size and strength. Scholars who see existing definitions as hurting women's ability to receive a fair trial propose modification of definitions of "imminence," expansion of the reasonable person doctrine to include the "reasonable battered woman," and elimination of duty to retreat.

Other scholars argue that existing self-defense doctrines can, in principle, accommodate battered women who kill their spouses. According to Professor Holly Maguigan, existing self-defense law is adequate if trial judges properly apply the laws to battered women who kill. Maguigan argues that the requirement that the threat to a defendant be imminent before she act in self-defense is not so limited that it prevent consideration of the woman's circumstances. Rather, a jury can and will consider the imminence requirement fulfilled when, for example, a woman kills her batterer with an honest and reasonable belief that the moment he wakes up he will kill her, and if she waits, she will be powerless to defend herself. Thus, Maguigan argues, existing definitions can accommodate the self-defense claim for battered women.

| "Despite Francine's acquittal, her femi-
nist supporters felt betrayed."

Abused Women Who Kill Are Not Weak

Evan Stark

After Francine Hughes burned her abusive husband to death in their bed, the defense won her an acquittal by convincing the jury that years of abuse and fear for her safety had driven her temporarily insane. Evan Stark, an associate professor in the School of Public Health at the University of Medicine & Dentistry of New Jersey, points out in the following piece that Hughes' feminist supporters resented the fact that the temporary insanity plea would make her and others like her appear crazy for killing their abusers. They wanted society to understand that women had a legitimate claim to self-defense if they feared their husbands threatened their lives.

The application of the vast edifice of research and helping services to relieve the personal suffering of abused persons is an important contribution to human progress. Despite this, the defense of abuse victims who kill or assault abusive partners continues to rely on the same basic legal fictions it did two centuries ago: sex-stereotyped notions of female weakness, insanity, self-defense of a victimized innocent against excessive brutality, and on the mixture of these views reflected in the battered woman's defense.

Evan Stark, *Coercive Control: The Entrapment of Women in Personal Life*. Oxford: Oxford University Press, 2007, pp. 148–151. Copyright © 2007 Oxford University Press. Reproduced by permission of Oxford University Press.

The Burning Bed Revisited

One hundred years after Fanny Hyde [a woman who killed her abusive employer in 1872] was acquitted, attorney Aryon Greydanus claimed that when Francine Hughes set fire to the bed in which her husband was sleeping, she was temporarily insane. . . .

For Michigan feminists, the years of abuse Francine endured epitomized the experiences of battered wives, and her dramatic response symbolized their justified right to defend themselves. Believing that a jury of her peers would readily accept Francine's response as rational, they urged her attorney to argue self-defense. But Greydanus worried that a self-defense plea would fail, largely because Mickey was asleep when Francine set the fire and so did not pose the imminent danger required by self-defense law. Instead, he stood with legal tradition and pled temporary insanity. As in Hyde's defense, the technical rationale for pleading temporary insanity was to make evidence of long-standing abuse admissible in court to establish what was going on that night in Francine's mind. . . .

The only evidence that Francine was insane was that the definitive step she had taken in resisting Mickey's abuse contrasted markedly with her earlier submissiveness. There was one significant difference between this defense and the arguments used to acquit the battered murderess in the nineteenth century. Greydanus argued that the battering itself caused Hughes to crack, not a predisposing frailty inherited with female gender.

Despite Francine's acquittal, her feminist supporters felt betrayed. The insanity label would stigmatize Francine, they argued, making it impossible to communicate why the country needed to act decisively to relieve the millions of women who faced a similar situation. Their concerns were unnecessary. In response to the verdict, *The Washington Post, Time, Newsweek,* and dozens of other publications complained that "the killing excuse" gave women a virtual license to retaliate and would most assuredly start a trend.

Should Women Be Measured by a Different Standard?

Editorial writers had reason to worry. Or so it appeared from the publicity given to the self-defense acquittals of Joan Little (1975), Inez Garcia (1977), and other women who killed men who sexually assaulted them shortly before or soon after Francine's act of defiance. These cases dramatized an important change in women's representation—the emergence of a feminist jurisprudence [body of law]. Three months before Hughes set fire to her house, feminist legal scholars Elizabeth Schneider and Nancy Stearns from the Center for Constitutional Law won a precedent-setting appeal from the Washington State Supreme Court that would have allowed Greydanus to claim self-defense simply because at the time of the fire, Hughes believed that the sleeping man posed a threat to her life.

Application of the "reasonable man" (or, later, "the reasonable person") standard in self-defense penalizes women in two ways: they are judged by an inappropriate masculine yardstick and their subjective perceptions are held to be irrelevant to the question of whether a theoretical reasonable person would have acted as she did. In appealing the Washington case, Schneider and her colleagues set the problem of reasonableness in the broader context of women's inequality.

The Washington case involved Yvonne Wanrow, who had wounded one attacker and killed another whom she believed to be a child molester and rapist. In her 1974 trial, Wanrow pleaded impaired mental state and self-defense. Despite the fact that the 5'4" woman was in a leg cast and walked with a crutch when she shot the 6'2" intoxicated intruder, she was sentenced to two twenty-year terms and one five-year term. In presenting what is known as the Wanrow jury instruction, the

Washington State Appeals Court overturned her conviction, holding that a woman's reasonable perception of danger may differ from a man's. The opinion emphasized both Wanrow's specific physical vulnerability due to her diminutive size and condition at the time of the attack and the special vulnerability that resulted because women as a class suffered the effects of sex discrimination. Wrote the court,

> The respondent was entitled to have the jury consider her actions in the light of her own perceptions of the situation, including those perceptions which were the product of our nation's long and unfortunate history of sex discrimination. . . . Until such time as the effects of that history are eradicated, care must be taken to assure that our self-defense instructions afford women the right to have their conduct judged in light of the individual physical handicaps which are the product of sex discrimination.

The assumption that "reasonable" women have a lower threshold of fear than men reflected the sexist ideology of an earlier epoch. But the Wanrow standard derived from a socio-historical analysis sympathetic to feminism and allowed a battered woman to claim self-defense even where her violence was preemptive or where she merely believed she would be attacked or killed if she failed to respond. The one prerequisite for using *Wanrow* was that the female defendant be identified with the historically victimized class.

CHAPTER 2

Police Are Not Obligated to Enforce Protection Orders

Case Overview

Town of Castle Rock, Colorado v. Gonzales (2005)

On the night of June 22, 1999, Jessica Gonzales repeatedly called the Castle Rock, Colorado, police to report that her estranged husband Simon Gonzales had kidnapped their three daughters from the front yard of her house. She had an order of protection filed with the police, which clearly specified that her husband must stay at least 100 yards from the house at all times or face immediate arrest. Despite her repeated appeals to the police to locate and arrest her husband, the police failed to act. Ultimately, Simon drove to the police station and fired a shot. After police returned fire, killing Simon, they found the bodies of the three girls in the back of his pickup. He had shot and killed each of them.

Jessica Gonzales filed suit against the police department of Castle Rock. She and her attorney maintained that in failing to carry out the terms of the order of protection, the police had denied her and her children their right to due process protected under the Fourteenth Amendment to the Constitution. Due process says that a person cannot be deprived of her right to property without the proper legal procedure. The property in question was the order of protection, which Gonzales' attorneys said that as a taxpaying citizen of Castle Rock she had every right to assume would be carried out. After a series of decisions and reversals, the full court of appeals ruled in Gonzales' favor.

The Castle Rock police department filed an appeal with the U.S. Supreme Court, who then had to decide whether an order of protection amounted to property. In other words, they had to decide whether Gonzales, her children, and other domestic violence victims had a legal right to police protection. In the summer of 2005, the Court's majority ruled that a protection order does not constitute property, so victims cannot seek protection under the Fourteenth Amendment's due process clause when police fail to enforce such an order. Justices insisted that police must always retain the ability to use their own discretion in deciding when and how to respond to a domestic violence call, even in a case where a protection order is on file. The Court's decision has not been overturned, nor has the precedent it set been altered in any way.

Critics decried *Castle Rock v. Gonzales* as one more in a series of decisions that erodes the rights of those who cannot protect themselves. It called into question, they said, the very purpose of orders of protection. Filing such an order has been a domestic violence victim's only real and legal means of protecting herself and her family against an abuser. Who, they ask, could blame her for taking the law into her own hands and resorting to physical violence?

Victims' rights advocates say that the crux of the problem is that police are understandably reluctant to respond to domestic violence calls. Such intervention can and often does result in further confusion, emotional outbursts, and physical violence. According to these advocates, rather than turning a blind eye to enforcement, municipalities must offer intensive training to help officers feel informed and prepared to respond to just this kind of potentially volatile situation.

> "A well established tradition of police
> discretion has long coexisted with ap-
> parently mandatory arrest statutes."

The Court's Decision:
Enforcement of a Protection
Order Is Not a Right

Antonin Scalia

*Jessica Gonzales sued the Castle Rock, Colorado, police depart-
ment on the grounds that in failing to enforce the restraining order she had against her husband, they violated her right to due
process, or consistent enforcement of a piece of legislation, secured by the Fourteenth Amendment to the Constitution.
Gonzales' husband murdered their three daughters before being
shot and killed by police. Although she won at the 10th Circuit
Court of Appeals, Gonzales lost at the Supreme Court. In the following opinion delivered by Justice Antonin Scalia, the majority
decided the case primarily on the basis that the protection order,
as written, did not constitute an actual property or right that
must be defended since enforcing it could be left to police discretion.*

The Fourteenth Amendment to the United States Constitution provides that a state shall not "deprive any person of
life, liberty, or property, without due process of law." In 42
U.S.C. §1983, Congress has created a federal cause of action
for "the deprivation of any rights, privileges, or immunities
secured by the Constitution and laws." Respondent claims the

Antonin Scalia, "Opinion of the Court," in *Town of Castle Rock, Colorado v. Certiorari
to the United States Court of Appeals for the 10th Circuit*, no. 04-278, March 21, 2005.

benefit of this provision on the ground that she had a property interest in police enforcement of the restraining order against her husband; and that the town deprived her of this property without due process by having a policy that tolerated nonenforcement of restraining orders. . . .

The procedural component of the Due Process Clause does not protect everything that might be described as a "benefit": "To have a property interest in a benefit, a person clearly must have more than an abstract need or desire" and "more than a unilateral expectation of it. He must, instead, have a legitimate claim of entitlement to it." Such entitlements are "'of course, . . . not created by the Constitution. Rather, they are created and their dimensions are defined by existing rules or understandings that stem from an independent source such as state law.'"

Protection Orders Are Not Legal Benefits

Our cases recognize that a benefit is not a protected entitlement if government officials may grant or deny it in their discretion. The Court of Appeals in this case determined that Colorado law created an entitlement to enforcement of the restraining order because the "court-issued restraining order . . . specifically dictated that its terms must be enforced" and a "state statute command[ed]" enforcement of the order when certain objective conditions were met (probable cause to believe that the order had been violated and that the object of the order had received notice of its existence). Respondent contends that we are obliged "to give deference to the Tenth Circuit's analysis of Colorado law on" whether she had an entitlement to enforcement of the restraining order.

We will not, of course, defer to the Tenth Circuit on the ultimate issue: whether what Colorado law has given respondent constitutes a property interest for purposes of the Fourteenth Amendment. That determination, despite its state-law underpinnings, is ultimately one of federal constitutional law.

"Although the underlying substantive interest is created by 'an independent source such as state law,' *federal constitutional law* determines whether that interest rises to the level of a 'legitimate claim of entitlement' protected by the Due Process Clause." Resolution of the federal issue begins, however, with a determination of what it is that state law provides. In the context of the present case, the central state-law question is whether Colorado law gave respondent a right to police enforcement of the restraining order. . . .

The Restraining Order Was Not Mandatory

The critical language in the restraining order came not from any part of the order itself (which was signed by the state-court trial judge and directed to the restrained party, respondent's husband), but from the preprinted notice to law-enforcement personnel that appeared on the back of the order. That notice effectively restated the statutory provision describing "peace officers' duties" related to the crime of violation of a restraining order. At the time of the conduct at issue in this case, that provision read as follows:

> "(a) Whenever a restraining order is issued, the protected person shall be provided with a copy of such order. *A peace officer shall use every reasonable means to enforce a restraining order.*

> "(b) *A peace officer shall arrest, or, if an arrest would be impractical under the circumstances, seek a warrant for the arrest of a restrained person* when the peace officer has information amounting to probable cause that:

> "(I) The restrained person has violated or attempted to violate any provision of a restraining order; and

> "(II) The restrained person has been properly served with a copy of the restraining order or the restrained person has received actual notice of the existence and substance of such order.

"(c) In making the probable cause determination described in paragraph (b) of this subsection (3), a peace officer shall assume that the information received from the registry is accurate. *A peace officer shall enforce a valid restraining order whether or not there is a record of the restraining order in the registry.*"

The Court of Appeals concluded that this statutory provision—especially taken in conjunction with a statement from its legislative history, and with another statute restricting criminal and civil liability for officers making arrests—established the Colorado Legislature's clear intent "to alter the fact that the police were not enforcing domestic abuse restraining orders," and thus its intent "that the recipient of a domestic abuse restraining order have an entitlement to its enforcement." Any other result, it said, "would render domestic abuse restraining orders utterly valueless."

This last statement is sheer hyperbole [exaggeration]. Whether or not respondent had a right to enforce the restraining order, it rendered certain otherwise lawful conduct by her husband both criminal and in contempt of court. The creation of grounds on which he could be arrested, criminally prosecuted, and held in contempt was hardly "valueless"— even if the prospect of those sanctions ultimately failed to prevent him from committing three murders and a suicide.

We do not believe that these provisions of Colorado law truly made enforcement of restraining orders *mandatory*. A well established tradition of police discretion has long coexisted with apparently mandatory arrest statutes. . . .

A true mandate of police action would require some stronger indication from the Colorado Legislature than "shall use every reasonable means to enforce a restraining order" (or even "shall arrest . . . or . . . seek a warrant") That language is not perceptibly more mandatory than the Colorado statute which has long told municipal chiefs of police that they "shall pursue and arrest any person fleeing from justice in any part of the state" and that they "shall apprehend any person in the act of committing any offense . . . and, forthwith and without any warrant, bring such person before a . . . competent authority for examination and trial." It is hard to imagine that a Colorado peace officer would not have some discretion to determine that—despite probable cause to believe a restraining order has been violated—the circumstances of the violation or the competing duties of that officer or his agency counsel decisively against enforcement in a particular instance. The practical necessity for discretion is particularly apparent in a case such as this one, where the suspected violator is not actually present and his whereabouts are unknown. ("There is a vast difference between a mandatory duty to arrest [a violator who is on the scene] and a mandatory duty to conduct a follow-up investigation [to locate an absent violator]. . . . A mandatory duty to investigate would be completely open-ended as to priority, duration and intensity"). . . .

Respondent does not specify the precise means of enforcement that the Colorado restraining-order statute assertedly mandated—whether her interest lay in having police arrest her husband, having them seek a warrant for his arrest, or having them "use every reasonable means, up to and including arrest, to enforce the order's terms." Such indeterminacy is not the hallmark of a duty that is mandatory. Nor can someone be safely deemed "entitled" to something when the identity of the alleged entitlement is vague. . . .

A Restraining Order Is Not Property

Respondent's alleged interest stems only from a state's *statutory* scheme—from a restraining order that was authorized by and tracked precisely the statute on which the Court of Appeals relied. She does not assert that she has any common-law or contractual entitlement to enforcement. If she was given a statutory entitlement, we would expect to see some indication of that in the statute itself. Although Colorado's statute spoke of "protected person[s]" such as respondent, it did so in connection with matters other than a right to enforcement. It said that a "protected person shall be provided with a copy of [a restraining] order" when it is issued, that a law enforcement agency "shall make all reasonable efforts to contact the protected party upon the arrest of the restrained person," and that the agency "shall give [to the protected person] a copy" of the report it submits to the court that issued the order. Perhaps most importantly, the statute spoke directly to the protected person's power to "initiate contempt proceedings against the restrained person if the order [was] issued in a civil action or request the prosecuting attorney to initiate contempt proceedings if the order [was] issued in a criminal action." The protected person's express power to "initiate" civil contempt proceedings contrasts tellingly with the mere ability to "request" initiation of criminal contempt proceedings—and even more dramatically with the complete silence about any power to "request" (much less demand) that an arrest be made.

The creation of a personal entitlement to something as vague and novel as enforcement of restraining orders cannot "simply g[o] without saying." We conclude that Colorado has not created such an entitlement.

Even if we were to think otherwise concerning the creation of an entitlement by Colorado, it is by no means clear that an individual entitlement to enforcement of a restraining order could constitute a "property" interest for purposes of the Due Process Clause. Such a right would not, of course, resemble any traditional conception of property. . . .

We conclude, therefore, that respondent did not, for purposes of the Due Process Clause, have a property interest in police enforcement of the restraining order against her husband. It is accordingly unnecessary to address the Court of Appeal's determination that the town's custom or policy prevented the police from giving her due process when they deprived her of that alleged interest.

> *"Recognizing respondent's property interest in the enforcement of her restraining order is fully consistent with our precedent."*

Dissenting Opinion: Enforcement of a Protection Order Is a Right

John Paul Stevens

In the following dissenting opinion, U.S. Supreme Court Justice Stevens maintains that the police department of Castle Rock Colorado violated Jessica Gonzales' and her children's right to due process under the Constitution. Due process means following the letter of a piece of legislation the same way in every case. Police chose not to enforce a protection order Gonzales had against her estranged husband, who murdered their three daughters before finally being shot and killed by police. Though the Court's majority ruled that, as written, the protection order did not constitute an actual property right, Stevens disagrees. He insists that Gonzales had as much right to expect police to enforce the protection order as she would have had she hired a private individual or company to protect her and her children.

Even if the Court had good reason to doubt the Court of Appeals' determination of state law, it would, in my judgment, be a far wiser course to certify the question to the Colorado Supreme Court. Powerful considerations support certification in this case. First, principles of federalism and co-

John Paul Stevens, "Dissenting Opinion," in *Town of Castle Rock, Colorado v. Certiorari to the United States Court of Appeals for the 10th Circuit*, no. 04-278, March 21, 2005.

mity [social harmony] favor giving a state's high court the opportunity to answer important questions of state law, particularly when those questions implicate uniquely local matters such as law enforcement and might well require the weighing of policy considerations for their correct resolution. . . . Second, by certifying a potentially dispositive state-law issue, the Court would adhere to its wise policy of avoiding the unnecessary adjudication of difficult questions of constitutional law. Third, certification would promote both judicial economy and fairness to the parties. After all, the Colorado Supreme Court is the ultimate authority on the meaning of Colorado law, and if in later litigation it should disagree with this Court's provisional state-law holding, our efforts will have been wasted and respondent will have been deprived of the opportunity to have her claims heard under the authoritative view of Colorado law. The unique facts of this case only serve to emphasize the importance of employing a procedure that will provide the correct answer to the central question of state law. . . .

A Question of Discretion

Three flaws in the Court's rather superficial analysis of the merits highlight the unwisdom of its decision to answer the state-law question *de novo* [starting afresh]. First, the Court places undue weight on the various statutes throughout the country that seemingly mandate police enforcement but are generally understood to preserve police discretion. As a result, the Court gives short shrift to the unique case of "mandatory arrest" statutes in the domestic violence context; states passed a wave of these statutes in the 1980s and 1990s with the unmistakable goal of eliminating police discretion in this area. Second, the Court's formalistic analysis fails to take seriously the fact that the Colorado statute at issue in this case was enacted for the benefit of the narrow class of persons who are beneficiaries of domestic restraining orders, and that the order at issue in this case was specifically intended to provide protection to respondent and her children. Finally, the Court is simply wrong to assert that a citizen's interest in the government's commitment to provide police enforcement in certain defined circumstances does not resemble any "traditional conception of property" in fact, a citizen's property interest in such a commitment is just as concrete and worthy of protection as her interest in any other important service the government or a private firm has undertaken to provide.

In 1994, the Colorado General Assembly passed omnibus legislation targeting domestic violence. The part of the legislation at issue in this case mandates enforcement of a domestic restraining order upon probable cause of a violation, while another part directs that police officers "shall, without undue delay, arrest" a suspect upon "probable cause to believe that a crime or offense of domestic violence has been committed." In adopting this legislation, the Colorado General Assembly joined a nationwide movement of states that took aim at the crisis of police underenforcement in the domestic violence sphere by implementing "mandatory arrest" statutes. The crisis of underenforcement had various causes, not least of which was the perception by police departments and police officers that domestic violence was a private, "family" matter and that arrest was to be used as a last resort. . . . In response to these realities, and emboldened by a well-known 1984 experiment by the Minneapolis police department, "many states enacted mandatory arrest statutes under which a police officer must arrest an abuser when the officer has probable cause to believe that a domestic assault has occurred or that a protection order has been violated." The purpose of these statutes was precisely to "counter police resistance to arrests in domestic violence cases by removing or restricting police officer discretion; mandatory arrest policies would increase police response and reduce batterer recidivism."

Thus, when Colorado passed its statute in 1994, it joined the ranks of fifteen states that mandated arrest for domestic violence offenses and nineteen states that mandated arrest for domestic restraining order violations.

Given the specific purpose of these statutes, there can be no doubt that the Colorado Legislature used the term "shall" advisedly in its domestic restraining order statute. While "shall" is probably best read to mean "may" in other Colorado statutes that seemingly mandate enforcement, it is clear that the elimination of police discretion was integral to Colorado and its fellow states' solution to the problem of underenforcement in domestic violence cases. Since the text of Colorado's statute perfectly captures this legislative purpose, it is hard to imagine what the Court has in mind when it insists on "some stronger indication from the Colorado Legislature." . . .

A Restraining Order Is a Clear Benefit

The Court suggests that the fact that "enforcement" may encompass different acts infects any entitlement to enforcement with "indeterminacy." But this objection is also unfounded. Our cases have never required the object of an entitlement to be some mechanistic, unitary thing. Suppose a state entitled every citizen whose income was under a certain level to receive health care at a state clinic. The provision of health care is not a unitary thing—doctors and administrators must decide what tests are called for and what procedures are required, and these decisions often involve difficult applications of judgment. But it could not credibly be said that a citizen lacks an entitlement to health care simply because the content of that entitlement is not the same in every given situation. Similarly, the enforcement of a restraining order is not some amorphous, indeterminate thing. Under the statute, if the police have probable cause that a violation has occurred, enforcement consists of either making an immediate arrest or seeking a warrant and then executing an arrest—traditional, well-defined tasks that law enforcement officers perform every day. . . .

Given that Colorado law has quite clearly eliminated the police's discretion to deny enforcement, respondent is correct that she had much more than a "unilateral expectation" that the restraining order would be enforced; rather, she had a "legitimate claim of entitlement" to enforcement. Recognizing respondent's property interest in the enforcement of her restraining order is fully consistent with our precedent. This Court has "made clear that the property interests protected by procedural due process extend well beyond actual ownership of real estate, chattels, or money." . . .

Police enforcement of a restraining order is a government service that is no less concrete and no less valuable than other government services, such as education. The relative novelty of recognizing this type of property interest is explained by the relative novelty of the domestic violence statutes creating a mandatory arrest duty; before this innovation, the unfettered discretion that characterized police enforcement defeated any citizen's "legitimate claim of entitlement" to this service. Novel or not, respondent's claim finds strong support in the principles that underlie our due process jurisprudence [body of law]. In this case, Colorado law *guaranteed* the provision of a certain service, in certain defined circumstances, to a certain class of beneficiaries, and respondent reasonably relied on that guarantee. As we observed in *Roth*, "[i]t is a purpose of the ancient institution of property to protect those claims upon which people rely in their daily lives, reliance that must not be arbitrarily undermined." Surely, if respondent had contracted with a private security firm to provide her and her daughters with protection from her husband, it would be apparent that she possessed a property interest in such a contract. Here, Colorado undertook a comparable obligation, and respondent—with restraining order in hand—justifiably relied on that undertaking. Respondent's claim of entitlement to this promised service is no less legitimate than the other claims our cases have upheld, and no less concrete than a hypothetical agreement with a private firm. The fact that it is based on a statutory enactment and a judicial order entered for her special protection, rather than on a formal contract, does not provide a principled basis for refusing to consider it "property" worthy of constitutional protection.

Police Were Negligent

Because respondent had a property interest in the enforcement of the restraining order, state officials could not deprive her of that interest without observing fair procedures. Her description of the police behavior in this case and the department's callous policy of failing to respond properly to reports of restraining order violations clearly alleges a due process violation. At the very least, due process requires that the relevant state decisionmaker *listen* to the claimant and then *apply the relevant criteria* in reaching his decision. The failure to observe these minimal procedural safeguards creates an unacceptable risk of arbitrary and "erroneous deprivation[s]." According to respondent's complaint—which we must construe liberally at this early stage in the litigation, the process she was afforded by the police constituted nothing more than a "'sham or a pretense.'"

Accordingly, I respectfully dissent.

> "Given the court's position that the po-
> lice are not obliged to protect us, re-
> sponsible adults need the ability to de-
> fend themselves."

The *Castle Rock v. Gonzales* Ruling Reveals the Need for Gun Ownership

Wendy McElroy

The U.S. Supreme Court ruled that the police department of the City of Castle Rock, Colorado, did not violate Jessica Gonzales' constitutional right to due process in failing to enforce a protection order against her estranged husband, who murdered their three children before finally being shot and killed by police. The ruling left many questioning what recourse vulnerable people have against those who would harm them. In the following piece, Canadian feminist author Wendy McElroy insists that gun control advocates do a disservice to battered women and other vulnerable adults by trying to keep guns out of everyone's hands. She maintains that if Jessica Gonzales had possessed a gun and been trained to use it, her children's murders might never have happened. McElroy is the editor of ifeminist.com *and is a research fellow for the Independent Institute, a political think tank.*

On June 27, in the case of *Castle Rock v. Gonzales*, the Supreme Court found that Jessica Gonzales did not have a constitutional right to police protection even in the presence of a restraining order.

By a vote of seven-to-two, the Supreme Court ruled that Gonzales has no right to sue her local police department for failing to protect her and her children from her estranged husband.

The post-mortem discussion on *Gonzales* has been fiery but it has missed an obvious point. If the government won't protect you, then you have to take responsibility for your own self-defense and that of your family. The Court's ruling is a sad decision, but one that every victim and/or potential victim of violence must note: calling the police is not enough. You must also be ready to defend yourself.

In 1999, Gonzales obtained a restraining order against her estranged husband Simon, which limited his access to their children. On June 22, 1999, Simon abducted their three daughters. Though the Castle Rock police department disputes some of the details of what happened next, the two sides are in basic agreement: After her daughters' abduction, Gonzales repeatedly phoned the police for assistance. Officers visited the home. Believing Simon to be non-violent and, arguably, in compliance with the limited access granted by the restraining order, the police did nothing.

The next morning, Simon committed "suicide by cop." He shot a gun repeatedly through a police station window and was killed by returned fire. The murdered bodies of Leslie, 7, Katheryn, 9, and Rebecca, 10, were found in Simon's pickup truck.

In her lawsuit, Gonzales claimed the police violated her Fourteenth Amendment right to due process and sued them for $30 million. She won at the Appeals level.

What were the arguments that won and lost in the Supreme Court? . . .

Police Have No Constitutional Obligation to Protect

Local officials fell back upon a rich history of court decisions that found the police to have no constitutional obligation to protect individuals from private individuals. In 1856, the U.S. Supreme Court (*South v. Maryland*) found that law enforcement officers had no affirmative duty to provide such protection. In 1982, (*Bowers v. DeVito*), the Court of Appeals, Seventh Circuit held, ". . . there is no Constitutional right to be protected by the state against being murdered by criminals or madmen."

Later court decisions have concurred. . . .

Anti-domestic violence advocates and women's groups, such as the National Association of Women Lawyers, failed to establish that restraining orders were constitutional entitlements. If they had succeeded, the enforcement of such orders would have been guaranteed by due process. Failure to enforce them would have been grounds for a lawsuit against the police, a precedent that local officials feared would flood them with expensive litigation.

Public analysis of *Rock v. Gonzales* has been largely defined by these two opposing positions. . . .

Given the court's position that the police are not obliged to protect us, responsible adults need the ability to defend themselves. Thus, no law or policy should impede the access to gun ownership.

Responsible adults—both male and female—have both a right and a need to defend themselves and their families, with lethal force if necessary. If domestic violence advocates had focused on putting a gun in Jessica's hand and training her to use it, then the three Gonzales children might still be alive. After all, Jessica knew where her husband was. Indeed, she informed the police repeatedly of his location.

The Answer to Domestic Violence Is Gun Ownership

Of course, the Gonzales case—in and of itself—presents difficulties for the use of armed force by private citizens. Would the same police who believed Simon Gonzales was not dangerous have believed Jessica to be justified in picking up a gun to protect her children from him? Would the police have charged her for use of a weapon? Regardless, these sticky debates would probably be taking place in the presence of three living children and not three dead ones.

Nevertheless, most anti-domestic violence advocates strenuously avoid gun ownership as a possible solution to domestic violence. Instead, they appeal for more police intervention even though the police have no obligation to provide protection.

When groups like the National Organization for Women (NOW) do focus on gun ownership, it is to make such statements as, "Guns and domestic violence make a lethal combination, injuring and killing women every day."

In short, NOW addresses the issue of gun ownership and domestic violence only in order to demand a prohibition on the ability of abusers—always defined as men—to own weapons.

That position may be defensible. But it ignores half of the equation. It ignores the need of potential victims to defend themselves and their families. Anti-domestic violence and women's groups create the impression that guns are always part of the problem and never part of the solution.

The current mainstream of feminism—from which most anti-domestic violence advocates proceed—is an expression of left liberalism. It rejects private solutions based on individual rights in favor of laws aimed at achieving social goals. A responsible individual holding a gun in self-defense does not fit their vision of society.

In the final analysis, such advocates do not trust the judgment of the women they claim to be defending. They do not believe that Jessica Gonzales' three children would have been safer with a mother who was armed and educated in gun use.

The clear message of *Gonzales* bears repeating because you will not hear it elsewhere. The police have no obligation to protect individuals who, therefore, should defend themselves. The content of state laws does not matter; by Colorado State law, the police are required to "use every reasonable means to enforce a protection order." The Supreme Court has ruled and that's that.

In the wake of *Gonzales*, every anti-domestic violence advocate should advise victims—male or female—to learn self-defense. They should lobby for the repeal of any law or policy that hinders responsible gun ownership.

The true meaning of being anti-domestic violence is to help victims out of their victimhood and into a position of power.

> *"Despite the Gonzales ruling, nothing has changed regarding issuance and enforcement of civil and criminal protection orders in the state of Colorado."*

Protection Orders Save Lives

Randy Saucedo

The U.S. Supreme Court ruled that the police department of Castle Rock, Colorado, did not violate Jessica Gonzales' constitutional right to due process when they chose not to enforce a protection order she had filed against her husband. He murdered their three daughters before finally being shot and killed by police. Understandably, the ruling caused great concern in Colorado that protection orders could do little to protect vulnerable people. In the following article, attorney and advocacy director of the Colorado Coalition Against Domestic Violence Randy Saucedo reassures readers of the lifesaving power and validity of protection orders. He also describes steps he and his organization have taken to teach Colorado police officers how to better enforce these orders.

A t issue in the Supreme Court case *Town of Castle Rock, Colorado v. Jessica Gonzales* was whether victims of domestic violence have the right to sue if their local governments fail to protect them and their children from batterers. The Supreme Court ruled that Jessica Gonzales could not sue her police department for the failure to enforce a protection order. There has been a great amount of legal analysis of this decision, but as victim advocates, it is important to remain focused on the usefulness of protection orders.

Randy Saucedo, "Responding to the *Gonzales Case*," *The Voice*, Colorado Coalition Against Domestic Violence, Summer 2005. www.ccdav.org. Reproduced by permission.

One of the tenets of victim advocacy is to provide safety planning for victims of domestic violence and their children; the use of protection orders is part of that plan. Today, every jurisdiction in the Union, Territory and Tribal Nation Court not only has the authority to issue an order of protection, but also is required by federal law to enforce orders issued by other jurisdictions. Despite the *Gonzales* ruling, nothing has changed regarding the issuance and enforcement of civil and criminal protection orders in the state of Colorado. Colorado state law regarding orders of protection have not changed. Colorado Coalition Against Domestic Violence [CCADV] is working to ensure the *Gonzales* ruling doesn't have a negative impact on the public and law enforcement perception of the effectiveness of protection orders in the state of Colorado.

In the wake of the *Gonzales* ruling, CCADV engaged in a public relations campaign to notify and remind the public of the usefulness of protection orders. We were also steadfast in our criticism of the Castle Rock police department in their response to Ms. Gonzales pleas for help that very tragic evening. We believe that had the police department taken her seriously and provided reasonable steps of enforcing her order, the murders may have been prevented

CCADV, like many other nonprofit advocacy groups in the nation, was part of the legal response and support of Ms. Gonzales' argument but were also progressive in reaching out to law enforcement to collaborate on this issue.

Prior to the Court's ruling, CCADV and Project Safeguard had partnered with the Denver police department to provide "Roll Call Trainings" to line officers on protection orders. The intent was to provide street officers with the recent changes in the law regarding protection orders, the current academic research on their effectiveness and the ramifications of the *Gonzales* ruling. Valerie Jarstad of Project Safeguard, Denver police detective Dave Belue and CCADV provided ten–twelve minute trainings at all six police substations, beginning sometimes at 6 A.M. and ending at midnight. The trainings were successful in not only the delivery of information, but also in the feedback received from officers about protection orders and their views on domestic violence.

Ruling Did Not Change Importance of Protection Orders

During our media response to the *Gonzales* case ruling, it was important to let the public know the usefulness and effectiveness of protection orders. Several academic studies, including one from the American Medical Association, revealed that women who obtained permanent orders were less likely to have further contact with the perpetrator or require police intervention than those women who did not receive an order. This was evident in a study done in the Seventeenth Judicial District in 2004.

As advocates, we know that protection orders are *part of a larger safety plan* and that protection orders alone may not stop the violence or contact from the abusers. We hear often of the failures of protection orders. Certainly, nothing may stop a determined criminal bent on committing a crime. However, most abusers, after being served with an order or having one sustained against them, will leave the victim alone.

Protection orders are a useful and viable option for victims of abuse and we must be vigilant in their use. Their success is based on their accessibility, their enforcement, and the support of the community. The failure of these orders is rooted in the myth that women only use them as revenge and that they are "only a piece of paper."

I remember a specific incident when I was advocating for a client and the judge told me that the order was only a piece of paper. My response was "Your Honor, so is the Constitution."

> "*Thus, the* Gonzales *decision expands an already large barrier preventing abused women from seeking police protection from their batterers.*"

The U.S. Supreme Court Stripped Domestic Abuse Victims of Protection

Tritia L. Yuen

The note and comment editor of the American University Law Review *and 2007 juris doctoral candidate, Tritia Yuen, believes the Supreme Court overstepped its traditional role and authority in its ruling against domestic abuse victim Jessica Gonzales in her suit against the Castle Rock, Colorado, police department. The Court decided that police had not violated Gonzales' and her children's constitutional right to due process when they failed to enforce a protective order she had against her estranged husband. Before finally being shot and killed by police, Gonzales' husband murdered their three daughters. Yuen says the Court's decision set an ominous precedent that would allow states to selectively enforce legislation that protects its most vulnerable citizens, especially victims of domestic violence.*

The Supreme Court's ruling in *Gonzales* has significant implications. The Supreme Court's shifting jurisprudence impairs legislatures' ability to enact effective legislation. It also restricts the protection that 42 U.S.C. § 1983 [which allows

Tritia L. Yuen, "No Relief: Understanding the Supreme Court's Decision in *Town of Castle Rock v. Gonzales* Through the Rights/Remedies Framework," *American University Law Review*, August 2006. www.wcl.american.edu. Copyright © 2006 American University Law Review. Reproduced by permission.

civil action for deprivation of rights] provides to private citizens when state laws fail to protect them. In addition, *Gonzales* has grave public policy implications for victims of domestic violence.

Therefore, this comment concludes that the Supreme Court should have granted Ms. Gonzales post-deprivation relief. Courts should hold police and other state actors responsible for not following procedures and uphold the relief provided by state legislation. Even if Colorado's statute opened up municipalities to too much liability, it is the responsibility of the legislature to amend the statute. The Supreme Court overreached its rights-determining role in ignoring the intent of the Colorado legislature.

The Ruling Weakens State's Ability to Protect People

The *Gonzales* decision takes away the core function of state and local legislatures to accomplish what they deem necessary to protect their citizens, even where there is no violation of the Constitution. The Supreme Court, pursuant to its judicial review powers, can overturn unconstitutional state legislation. However, many experts question the Court's overreaching application of this power. Justice Breyer cautions the Court from overreaching, noting that "within the bounds of the rational, Congress, not the courts, must remain primarily responsible for striking the appropriate state/federal balance." Justice Breyer also criticizes the Court's increased willingness to overturn state legislation, even where there is clear legislative intent.

While the Court did not expressly invalidate section 18-6-805.5(3) of the Colorado Code, *Gonzales* eliminated the legislature's intent for mandatory enforcement. As police are not required to enforce [Temporary Restraining Orders] TROs, many fear that the orders are now useless. Accordingly, Justice Stevens' dissenting opinion in *Gonzales* emphasizes how the majority overstepped its role in deciding a state-law issue and strayed from the "tradition of judicial restraint."

As the rights/remedies framework explains, legislatures are best situated to consider the impact of their legislation, and courts are better situated to consider whether such legislation violates a right. Some scholars warn that serious consequences arise when courts overstep their rights-determining role. Courts enter the realm of deciding public policy, rather than properly interpreting and applying the law. If the judiciary continues in this direction, it can interpret what is mandatory as "not mandatory" at will, without any checks from the other branches of government. This is inappropriate because it allows courts too much power and takes away from the proper role of legislatures to balance public opinion with the protection of rights. This will leave many, like Ms. Gonzales, with no relief.

Finally, even if the Supreme Court had held the town of Castle Rock liable, it is the legislature's role to determine whether there is an unacceptable level of liability for state actors. If this is the case, the legislature should amend section 18-6-805.5(3) to create more discretion or shield police from liability. Moreover, it is beyond the Court's function to address its concern about exposing state actors to too much liability. *Gonzales* demonstrates the Court's unwillingness to trust legislatures to control the impact of their own legislation.

The Supreme Court's analysis in *Gonzales* also has important implications for other 42 U.S.C. § 1983 claims. Cases asking the Supreme Court to find a property entitlement interest are brought under § 1983 because it allows citizens to sue state actors for deprivation of a protected right. Section 1983 opens the door for liability where a state actor "subjects . . . any citizen of the United States . . . to the deprivation of any rights, privileges, or immunities secured by the Constitution and laws." In denying Ms. Gonzales relief, the Supreme Court severely limited the ability of § 1983 to protect private citizens. . . .

Ruling Makes Domestic Violence Victims Even More Vulnerable

Gonzales also creates considerable concern because of its public policy implications. Domestic violence is the number one cause of injury to women, and police protection is critical to protecting battered women and children. Experts believe that women are hesitant to seek police protection and will do so only if they believe that the police in fact will protect them. Moreover, women of color, like Ms. Gonzales, are the least likely group to seek police intervention because of a cultural distrust of police. Thus, the *Gonzales* decision expands an already large barrier preventing abused women from seeking police protection from their batterers. Domestic violence advocates, who have spent years convincing abused women to come forward for protection, can no longer guarantee that the state has a duty to protect women from their abusers.

Moreover, by deciding that police need not enforce protection orders, the Court endangers other vulnerable members of society who depend on restraining orders. Victims are now more likely to seek private methods of protection because they cannot rely on the state to protect them. Thus, the poor who cannot afford private security will be left especially vulnerable. Additionally, senior citizens, who are the "truly forgotten victims of domestic violence," will be affected disproportionately by discretionary enforcement of restraining orders.

As the Supreme Court has removed what is often a domestic violence victim's last hope for protection, the state's overall burden for protecting citizens will increase.... State responsibility exists only in cases of physical custody. Therefore, victims may seek custodial situations for protection even where a less extreme solution may be available. In addition, citizens may be more likely to seek private actions through tort [wrongful act] remedies against government actors. Overall, the *Gonzales* decision leaves the most vulnerable citizens at greater risk and encourages them to carry out acts that trained police officers are better suited to perform.

Police Violated the Victim's Right to Due Process

Ms. Gonzales and other advocates wanted the Supreme Court to hold Castle Rock police accountable for not following the procedures required by Section 18-6-805.5(3) of the Colorado Code. In *Gonzales*, there was substantial evidence that would lead a reasonable police officer to believe Mr. Gonzales violated the TRO. The police officers had affirmative knowledge that Mr. Gonzales had the girls, knowledge of his location, and Ms. Gonzales' called them repeatedly over six hours. Moreover, the Colorado court granted the TRO initially because it believed that Mr. Gonzales posed an imminent danger to Ms. Gonzales and her daughters. Therefore, the police officers' unwillingness to take any action fell short of the standard response of a reasonably well-trained officer.

The Fourteenth Amendment, which forbids deprivation of property without "due process of law," would have granted Ms. Gonzales a cause of action had the Court properly recognized Ms. Gonzales' property interest in the TRO's enforcement. In *Goss v. Lopez*, the Court clarified that sufficient procedural due process for property deprivation occurs when the state affords a citizen "*some* kind of notice" and "*some* kind of hearing." "*Some* kind of notice" and "*some* kind of hearing" does not place the burden on police to protect every victim. Rather, notice is satisfied where the police sufficiently follow standard procedures for responding to a TRO violation. Therefore, as soon as Ms. Gonzales confirmed Mr. Gonzales' violation of the TRO, the police should have located him and taken him into custody. Later, they could have applied discretion as to whether to file a motion of contempt against Mr. Gonzales. As such, the Court failed to protect Ms. Gonzales' procedural due process rights.

Since Colorado police failed to follow proper TRO enforcement procedures, the Court should have granted Ms. Gonzales post-deprivation relief. In *Parratt v. Taylor*, the Court recognized that post-deprivation relief could be required of states in instances of due process violations. Though the Court has not given a clear or consistent formulation of what constitutes sufficient post-deprivation relief, it has deferred to established state procedures. Thus, given Colorado state law, the Castle Rock police department should have sanctioned the individual officers named by Ms. Gonzales, and the state should have granted Ms. Gonzales compensation for her loss.

Given the Supreme Court's decision in *Gonzales*, states seeking to provide greater protections for victims of domestic violence should not focus exclusively on enacting mandatory enforcement statutes. Rather, they should promote greater cooperation between law enforcement and domestic violence social service providers. Collaborative efforts will hold police accountable through public pressure and awareness. Over time, strong collaboration will help domestic violence victims and advocates learn to trust that police will do the right thing, which will then encourage victims to seek help. As police are trained by domestic violence advocates to better identify well-founded fears and legitimate complaints, the overall effectiveness of police departments and the safety of women and children will improve.

In addition, states should bolster funding to address domestic violence. Many women stay in abusive relationships because they fear they will have no financial support if they leave. Therefore, states should increase financial assistance for domestic violence survivors. This creates incentives for women to seek police involvement, even though the state cannot require police to respond to TRO violations.

Finally, victims' advocates must increase publicity about police failure to enforce restraining orders. Increased publicity will put pressure on police to respond effectively to reports of

TRO violations, even if the law does not require them to do so. As police respond, they will rebuild trust with the community, and women will find the confidence to leave violent situations knowing that the police will protect them.

The Ruling Has Negative Implications

In *Gonzales*, the Supreme Court's departure from its traditional analysis recognizing and protecting entitlement property interests left Ms. Gonzales with no relief. The rights/remedies framework provides a tool for understanding this departure. Specifically, the Court overstepped its proper role of determining the extent and limit of legal rights to addressing the remedial concerns arising from the protection of rights. Thus, the Court showed that it is willing to shield states from liability, even when this requires ignoring a statute's plain language and clear legislative history. The Court's concern with the remedial impact of its decision explains why it failed to recognize Ms. Gonzales' property entitlement interest in TRO enforcement.

Gonzales represents the Supreme Court expanding its judicial review powers and exhibiting less and less restraint in overturning both state and federal legislation. This trend creates significant concerns as it reduces the ability of legislatures to protect their citizens and renders 42 U.S.C. § 1983 ineffective in holding state actors personally accountable for violating a private citizen's rights. Further, *Gonzales* leaves battered women, children, the poor, and the elderly at risk with no assurance of police protection. Communities and advocates must now exert stronger pressure on judges to prevent courts from overstepping their judicial review powers. Communities and advocates must also increase accountability for police through non-legislative means and encourage increased funding for support services to battered women. This will help victims of domestic violence who rely on protection orders feel empowered to leave violent situations and regain confidence that police will protect them.

CHAPTER 3

Using Out-of-Court
Statements as Testimony

Case Overview

Adrian Martell Davis v. Washington and *Hershel Hammon v. Indiana* (2006)

At stake in the combined 2006 domestic violence cases of *Davis v. Washington* and *Hammon v. Indiana* was whether out-of-court statements made by victims of domestic violence are admissible in court without the woman being present for cross-examination. Both alleged abusers had appealed their original guilty verdicts because their accusers failed to appear in court to verify their statements about the domestic violence. The defense attorneys representing the two men argued that unless the victims appeared in court to directly accuse them, the men's Sixth Amendment right to confrontation would be violated.

Though the two cases varied only slightly, a majority of Supreme Court justices viewed them quite differently. In *Davis v. Washington*, justices had to determine if a call that Adrian Davis's former girlfriend Michelle McCottrey made to a 911 operator while he beat her was admissible in court even though she hadn't appeared. Police interviewed domestic violence victim Amy Hammon after an incident with her husband Hershel had already occurred. In *Hammon v. Indiana*, the Court had to determine whether this interview could be used as evidence in her husband's trial though she hadn't been present for cross-examination. The justices based their opinion on whether the statements constituted testimony. For her testimonial statement to be admissible in court, an accuser must, the justices said, be present at trial. The Court's majority ruled that in *Davis v. Washington*, the 911 call was not testimony because, in it, McCottrey simply reported events as they occurred. They rejected Washington's appeal that his Sixth Amendment rights had been violated because McCottrey did not appear at trial for cross-examination. However, in *Hammon v. Indiana*, the majority ruled that, by agreeing to an interview with police, Amy Hammon had attempted to prove that the past events she described had occurred and had, therefore, given a testimonial statement meant to establish his guilt. By not appearing in court, she had violated her husband's Sixth Amendment right to confrontation. The Supreme Court granted Hershel Hammon his appeal.

The decisions in *Davis* and *Hammon* aroused almost universal condemnation. Many legal analysts criticized them because they were based on such a confusing and flimsy distinction between testimonial and nontestimonial statements. Instead of further clarifying the meaning of the words "testimony" and "witness," the Court had muddied them. The rulings offered little concrete guidance to lower courts as to what statements to allow in similar cases.

Feminist legal scholars said something far more dangerous had occurred as a result of the decisions; *Davis* and *Hammon* had set a terrible precedent in the arena of victim's rights. Many women feel too intimidated to face their abuser in court. By ruling in favor of Hershel Hammon, the Supreme Court, these critics maintain, went to greater lengths to protect a victimizer than his victim. Unless the decisions are overturned, these critics say they will loom over women who fear that their accusations against their abusers will not be allowed in court unless they conquer their fears of retaliation and publicly testify against their abusers.

> "No 'witness' goes into court to proclaim
> an emergency and seek help."

The Court's Decision: Distinctions Must Be Made Between Types of Out-of-Court Statements

Antonin Scalia

At issue in Davis v. Washington *and* Hammon v. Indiana *is whether 911 calls (*Davis*) or informal police interviews (*Hammon*) with domestic violence victims constitute testimony. If their statements are defined as testimony and used in a trial, the domestic violence victims must appear in court to protect the right of the accused to confrontation under the Sixth Amendment to the Constitution. The following majority opinion delivered by Supreme Court Justice Antonin Scalia declares that a 911 call does not constitute testimony because it describes current circumstances; it does not prove what happened in the past. On the other hand, the police interview in* Hammon *was given as evidence of a past crime and so was considered testimony. Where Davis's wife did not have to appear in court to have her 911 call admissible, the Court ruled that Hammon's wife must appear in court to confront her husband.*

These cases require us to determine when statements made to law enforcement personnel during a 911 call or at a crime scene are "testimonial" and thus subject to the requirements of the Sixth Amendment's Confrontation Clause.

Antonin Scalia, "Opinion of the Court in *Davis v. Washington* on Writ of Certiorari to the Supreme Court of Washington, and *Hammon v. Indiana* on Writ of Certiorari to the Supreme Court of Indiana," June 18, 2006.

The relevant statements in *Davis v. Washington* were made to a 911 emergency operator on February 1, 2001. When the operator answered the initial call, the connection terminated before anyone spoke. She reversed the call, and Michelle McCottry answered. In the ensuing conversation, the operator ascertained that McCottry was involved in a domestic disturbance with her former boyfriend Adrian Davis, the petitioner in this case:

911 Operator: Hello.

Complainant: Hello.

What's going on?

He's here jumpin' on me again.

Okay. Listen to me carefully. Are you in a house or an apartment?

I'm in a house.

Are there any weapons?

No. He's usin' his fists.

Okay. Has he been drinking?

No.

Okay, sweetie. I've got help started. Stay on the line with me, okay?

I'm on the line.

Listen to me carefully. Do you know his last name?

It's Davis.

Davis? Okay, what's his first name?

Adran.

What is it?

Adrian.

Adrian?

Yeah.

Okay. What's his middle initial?

Martell. He's runnin' now.

As the conversation continued, the operator learned that Davis had "just r[un] out the door" after hitting McCottry, and that he was leaving in a car with someone else. McCottry started talking, but the operator cut her off, saying, "Stop talking and answer my questions." She then gathered more information about Davis (including his birthday), and learned that Davis had told McCottry that his purpose in coming to the house was "to get his stuff," since McCottry was moving. McCottry described the context of the assault, after which the operator told her that the police were on their way. "They're gonna check the area for him first," the operator said, "and then they're gonna come talk to you."

McCottry Gave Information Under Stress

The police arrived within four minutes of the 911 call and observed McCottry's shaken state, the "fresh injuries on her forearm and her face," and her "frantic efforts to gather her belongings and her children so that they could leave the residence."

The State charged Davis with felony violation of a domestic no-contact order. "The State's only witnesses were the two police officers who responded to the 911 call. Both officers testified that McCottry exhibited injuries that appeared to be recent, but neither officer could testify as to the cause of the injuries." McCottry presumably could have testified as to whether Davis was her assailant, but she did not appear. Over Davis's objection, based on the Confrontation Clause of the Sixth Amendment, the trial court admitted the recording of her exchange with the 911 operator, and the jury convicted him. The Washington Court of Appeals affirmed. The Supreme Court of Washington, with one dissenting justice, also affirmed, concluding that the portion of the 911 conversation in which McCottry identified Davis was not testimonial, and that if other portions of the conversation were testimonial, admitting them was harmless beyond a reasonable doubt.

In *Hammon v. Indiana*, police responded late on the night of February 26, 2003, to a "reported domestic disturbance" at the home of Hershel and Amy Hammon. They found Amy alone on the front porch, appearing "'somewhat frightened,'" but she told them that "'nothing was the matter.'" She gave them permission to enter the house, where an officer saw "a gas heating unit in the corner of the living room" that had "flames coming out of the . . . partial glass front. There were pieces of glass on the ground in front of it and there was flame emitting from the front of the heating unit."

Hershel, meanwhile, was in the kitchen. He told the police "that he and his wife had 'been in an argument' but 'everything was fine now' and the argument 'never became physical.'" By this point Amy had come back inside. One of the officers remained with Hershel; the other went to the living room to talk with Amy, and "again asked [her] what had occurred." Hershel made several attempts to participate in Amy's conversation with the police but was rebuffed. The officer later testified that Hershel "became angry when I insisted that [he] stay separated from Mrs. Hammon so that we can investigate what had happened." After hearing Amy's account, the officer "had her fill out and sign a battery affidavit." Amy handwrote the following: "Broke our Furnace & shoved me down on the floor into the broken glass. Hit me in the chest and threw me down. Broke our lamps & phone. Tore up my van where I couldn't leave the house. Attacked my daughter."

Lower Courts Ruled Hammon Also Made "Excited Utterances"

The State charged Hershel with domestic battery and with violating his probation. Amy was subpoenaed, but she did not appear at his subsequent bench trial. The State called the officer who had questioned Amy, and asked him to recount what Amy told him and to authenticate the affidavit. Hershel's counsel repeatedly objected to the admission of this evidence. At one point, after hearing the prosecutor defend the affidavit because it was made "under oath," defense counsel said, "That doesn't give us the opportunity to cross-examine [the] person who allegedly drafted it. Makes me mad." Nonetheless, the trial court admitted the affidavit as a "present sense impression" and Amy's statements as "excited utterances" that "are expressly permitted in these kinds of cases even if the declarant is not available to testify." The officer thus testified that Amy

> "informed me that she and Hershel had been in an argument. That he became irrate [sic] over the fact of their daughter going to a boyfriend's house. The argument became ... physical after being verbal and she informed me that Mr. Hammon, during the verbal part of the argument was breaking things in the living room and I believe she stated he broke the phone, broke the lamp, broke the front of the heater. When it became physical he threw her down into the glass of the heater.

> "She informed me Mr. Hammon had pushed her onto the ground, had shoved her head into the broken glass of the heater and that he had punched her in the chest twice I believe."

The trial judge found Hershel guilty on both charges and the Indiana Court of Appeals affirmed in relevant part. The Indiana Supreme Court also affirmed, concluding that Amy's statement was admissible for state-law purposes as an excited utterance; that "a 'testimonial' statement is one given or taken in significant part for purposes of preserving it for potential future use in legal proceedings," where "the motivations of the questioner and declarant are the central concerns"; and that Amy's oral statement was not "testimonial" under these standards. It also concluded that, although the affidavit was testimonial and thus wrongly admitted, it was harmless beyond a reasonable doubt, largely because the trial was to the bench. . . .

Most of the American cases applying the Confrontation Clause or its state constitutional or common-law counterparts involved testimonial statements of the most formal sort— sworn testimony in prior judicial proceedings or formal depositions under oath—which invites the argument that the scope of the Clause is limited to that very formal category. But the English cases that were the progenitors [originators] of the Confrontation Clause did not limit the exclusionary rule to prior court testimony and formal depositions. In any event, we do not think it conceivable that the protections of the Confrontation Clause can readily be evaded by having a note-taking policeman *recite* the unsworn hearsay testimony of the declarant, instead of having the declarant sign a deposition. Indeed, if there is one point for which no case—English or early American, state or federal—can be cited, that is it.

Were Statements Testimonial?

The question before us in *Davis*, then, is whether, objectively considered, the interrogation that took place in the course of the 911 call produced testimonial statements. When we said in that "interrogations by law enforcement officers fall squarely within [the] class" of testimonial hearsay, we had immediately in mind (for that was the case before us) interrogations solely directed at establishing the facts of a past crime, in order to identify (or provide evidence to convict) the perpetrator. The product of such interrogation, whether reduced to a writing signed by the declarant or embedded in the memory (and perhaps notes) of the interrogating officer, is testimonial. It is, in the terms of the 1828 American dictionary quoted in *Crawford*, "'[a] solemn declaration or affirmation made for the purpose of establishing or proving some fact.'" . . . A 911 call, on the other hand, and at least the initial interrogation conducted in connection with a 911 call, is ordinarily not designed primarily to "establis[h] or prov[e]" some past fact, out to describe current circumstances requiring police assistance.

The difference between the interrogation in *Davis* and the one in *Crawford* is apparent on the face of things. In *Davis*, McCottry was speaking about events as *they were actually happening*, rather than "describ[ing] past events". Sylvia Crawford's interrogation, on the other hand, took place hours after the events she described had occurred. Moreover, any reasonable listener would recognize that McCottry (unlike Sylvia Crawford) was facing an ongoing emergency. Although one *might* call 911 to provide a narrative report of a crime absent any imminent danger, McCottry's call was plainly a call for help against bona fide physical threat. Third, the nature of what was asked and answered in *Davis*, again viewed objectively, was such that the elicited statements were necessary to be able to *resolve* the present emergency, rather than simply to learn (as in *Crawford*) what had happened in the past. That is true even of the operator's effort to establish the identity of the assailant, so that the dispatched officers might know whether they would be encountering a violent felon. And finally, the difference in the level of formality between the two interviews is striking. Crawford was responding calmly, at the station house, to a series of questions, with the officer-interrogator taping and making notes of her answers; McCottry's frantic answers were provided over the phone, in an environment that was not tranquil, or even (as far as any reasonable 911 operator could make out) safe.

We conclude from all this that the circumstances of McCottry's interrogation objectively indicate its primary purpose was to enable police assistance to meet an ongoing emergency. She simply was not acting as *a witness*; she was not *testifying*. What she said was not "a weaker substitute for live testimony" at trial. . . . No "witness" goes into court to proclaim an emergency and seek help. . . .

Determining the testimonial or non-testimonial character of the statements that were the product of the interrogation in *Hammon* is a much easier task, since they were not much different from the statements we found to be testimonial in *Crawford*. It is entirely clear from the circumstances that the interrogation was part of an investigation into possibly criminal past conduct—as, indeed, the testifying officer expressly acknowledged. There was no emergency in progress; the interrogating officer testified that he had heard no arguments or crashing and saw no one throw or break anything. When the officers first arrived, Amy told them that things were fine, and there was no immediate threat to her person. When the officer questioned Amy for the second time, and elicited the challenged statements, he was not seeking to determine (as in *Davis*) "what is happening," but rather "what happened." Objectively viewed, the primary, if not indeed the sole, purpose of the interrogation was to investigate a possible crime—which is, of course, precisely what the officer *should* have done. . . .

Respondents in both cases, joined by a number of their *amici* [uninvolved professional allowed to speak at a trial to provide related information], contend that the nature of the offenses charged in these two cases—domestic violence—requires greater flexibility in the use of testimonial evidence. This particular type of crime is notoriously susceptible to intimidation or coercion of the victim to ensure that she does not testify at trial. When this occurs, the Confrontation Clause gives the criminal a windfall. We may not, however, vitiate [impair] constitutional guarantees when they have the effect of allowing the guilty to go free. But when defendants seek to undermine the judicial process by procuring or coercing silence from witness and victims, the Sixth Amendment does not require courts to acquiesce. While defendants have no duty to assist the State in proving their guilt, they *do* have the duty to refrain from acting in ways that destroy the integrity of the criminal-trial system. We reiterate what we said in *Crawford:* that "the role of forfeiture by wrongdoing . . . extinguishes confrontation claims on essentially equitable grounds." That is, one who obtains the absence of a witness by wrongdoing forfeits the constitutional right to confrontation.

> "The Court's determination that the evidence against Hammon must be excluded extends the Confrontation Clause far beyond the abuses it was intended to prevent."

Dissenting Opinion: Out-of-Court Statements Can Be Used as Evidence

Clarence Thomas

A majority of Supreme Court justices ruled in the combined domestic violence case of Davis v. Washington *(911 call) and* Hammon v. Indiana *(police interview) that a 911 call reporting an emergency is admissible in court as evidence while a police interview with a victim is not. If verbal evidence is considered testimony, then the victim must appear in court to confront her abuser under the Confrontation Clause of the Constitution. In the following dissenting opinion, Justice Clarence Thomas disagreed that a police interview after an attack should be considered testimony while a 911 call was not. Law enforcement took accounts from these women to assess whether their assailants still represented a threat to them, which, Thomas says, both men undoubtedly did. Given this, he asserts that regardless of when the accounts were taken, they should be admissible in court without the victims' presence.*

Clarence Thomas, "Dissenting Opinion: *Davis v. Washington* on Writ of Certiorari to the Supreme Court of Washington and *Hammon v. Indiana* on Writ of Certiorari to the Supreme Court of Indiana," June 18, 2006.

Neither the 911 call at issue in *Davis* nor the police questioning at issue in *Hammon* is testimonial under the appropriate framework. Neither the call nor the questioning is itself a formalized dialogue. Nor do any circumstances surrounding the taking of the statements render those statements sufficiently formal . . . the statements were neither Mirandized [person formally reminded of their right to remain silent or to have an attorney present] nor custodial, nor accompanied by any similar indicia of formality. Finally, there is no suggestion that the prosecution attempted to offer the women's hearsay evidence at trial in order to evade confrontation. Accordingly, the statements at issue in both cases are nontestimonial and admissible under the Confrontation Clause.

Courts Should Not Have to Guess

The Court's determination that the evidence against Hammon must be excluded extends the Confrontation Clause far beyond the abuses it was intended to prevent. When combined with the Court's holding that the evidence against Davis is perfectly admissible, however, the Court's *Hammon* holding also reveals the difficulty of applying the Court's requirement that courts investigate the "primary purpose[s]" of the investigation. The Court draws a line between the two cases based on its explanation that *Hammon* involves "no emergency in progress," but instead, mere questioning as "part of an investigation into possibly criminal past conduct," and its explanation that *Davis* involves questioning for the "primary purpose" of "enabl[ing] police assistance to meet an ongoing emergency." But the fact that the officer in *Hammon* was investigating Mr. Hammon's past conduct does not foreclose the possibility that the primary purpose of his inquiry was to assess whether Mr. Hammon constituted a continuing danger to his wife, requiring further police presence or action. It is hardly remarkable that Hammon did not act abusively towards his wife in the presence of the officers, and his good judgment to refrain from criminal behavior in the presence of police sheds little, if any, light on whether his violence would have resumed had the police left without further questioning, transforming what the Court dismisses as "past conduct" back into an "ongoing emergency." Nor does the mere fact that Mc-Cottry needed emergency aid shed light on whether the "primary purpose" of gathering, for example, the name of her assailant was to protect the police, to protect the victim, or to gather information for prosecution. In both of the cases before the Court, like many similar cases, pronouncement of the "primary" motive behind the interrogation calls for nothing more than a guess by courts.

Because the standard adopted by the Court today is neither workable nor a targeted attempt to reach the abuses forbidden by the [Confrontation] Clause, I concur only in the judgment in *Davis v. Washington* and respectfully dissent from the Court's resolution of *Hammon v. Indiana.*

> *"Any test that allows an un-cross-examined 911 call as evidence to convict is simply wrong."*

The Supreme Court Has Confused the Testimony Issue in Cases of Abuse

Craig M. Bradley

The Supreme Court's majority opinion in combined domestic violence cases Davis v. Washington *and* Hammon v. Indiana *set a confusing precedent for lower courts to follow, according to Craig M. Bradley, law professor at Indiana University. The Court ruled that the 911 call in* Davis *was not testimony while the police interview in* Hammon *was. If an account is testimony, then the person who gave it must appear in court to confront the accused abuser under the Constitution's Confrontation Clause. Bradley maintains here that the Court's means of determining testimony—whether the statement was given during the abuse (non-testimonial) or after (testimonial)—is too difficult to ascertain. He insists that eyewitness statements, such as those both of these women gave, should always be considered testimonial because useful information can be gained during cross-examination. Bradley suggests that witness reliability would be a better determiner of testimony than when a person's account was taken.*

In a combined case, *Davis v. Washington* and *Hammon v. Indiana*, the Supreme Court answered a tricky question about the Sixth Amendment's Confrontation Clause that had bedeviled the lower courts. The issue was whether a 911 call (in *Davis*) and a police interview with a witness (in *Hammon*) were "testimonial." If so, then they couldn't be used at the defendants' trials without the witnesses testifying.

The Court, in an 8–1 decision written by Justice Antonin Scalia, concluded that the 911 call was not testimonial but the police interview was. This ruling only furthers the confusion over the "testimonial/non-testimonial" dichotomy the Court created in its decision in *Crawford v. Washington* two years ago.

In *Crawford*, a defendant's conviction for assault was based partly on a statement his wife made to police officers. She did not testify at trial. In striking down *Crawford's* conviction, the Court overruled *Ohio v. Roberts*, which had found that hearsay statements did not violate the Confrontation Clause if they fell under a "firmly rooted hearsay exception" or had other "adequate indicia [indicator] of reliability." Applying *Roberts*, the state courts had admitted the wife's statement on the grounds that it appeared reliable because it corresponded closely to what the defendant had said.

But in *Crawford*, the Supreme Court said that "reliability" was no longer the appropriate test; instead, courts must determine whether a statement is "testimonial."

Finding the Constitutional Framers' Intent

The Confrontation Clause was intended to curb the use of evidence allegedly given to investigating magistrates by witnesses who did not appear at trial. But the historical law the Court cites in *Crawford* supports only the proposition that no hearsay evidence could be used against a defendant. This proposition runs counter to historical fact.

Indeed, the *Crawford* Court boldly declared—without any historical support—that "not all hearsay implicates the Sixth Amendment's core concerns. An off-hand, overheard remark might not be unreliable evidence. . . ." Why not? Well, the

Court reasoned circularly, because it is not testimonial, and only testimonial evidence concerned the framers.

Dissenting in *Crawford*, Chief Justice William Rehnquist, joined by Justice Sandra Day O'Connor, pointed out that "the Court's distinction between testimonial and non-testimonial statements . . . is no better rooted in history than our current doctrine." There was apparently no consistent rule, he wrote, and hearsay was "often heard by the jury." In fact, the most clearly testimonial statements—those taken by magistrates under oath—were the most likely to be admitted. Because of this, Rehnquist concluded that the old rule was correct, and the statement by Crawford's wife was admissible.

Other than statements made under oath, it is unclear which statements are testimonial and which are not. Contrary to the historical evidence Rehnquist presented, only non-testimonial statements are now admissible in the absence of the declarant [person making a statement]. Crawford held that a statement given to police officers after they issued Miranda [legal right of a person to remain silent and to have an attorney] warnings was sufficiently formal to count as testimonial. But what about the 911 call in *Davis*, and the non-Mirandized statements in *Hammon*?

Before discussing the Court's answer, it is helpful to consider an alternate approach. Given that the history on this question is fuzzy, isn't "reliability" a better standard? While often inconsistent and confusing, reliability at least presents a sensible target. Instead, courts must now define "non-testimonial"—a target that is equally hard to hit and that makes no sense, historically or otherwise.

Take 911 calls. They are inherently unreliable. People who make them are usually upset and prone to the type of overstatement that calls out for cross-examination: "Now, when you told the operator, 'He's trying to kill me,' you didn't really think he was trying to kill you, did you?" Yet *Davis/Hammon* concludes that such non-testimonial statements may be used against a defendant without the declarant testifying.

Oddly, under the old hearsay rules, which Rehnquist advanced, such a statement was also admissible as a spontaneous utterance. The theory was that spontaneous utterances are less likely to be calculated lies—which is true, but they're also more likely to be exaggerated or mistaken, and even more likely than calculated lies to be repudiated on cross [examination]. . . .

And what about the non-Mirandized statement? In *Davis/ Hammon*, the Court found that it is testimonial—and therefore can't be used to obtain a conviction. It is not clear whether such a statement would have been admissible under the old rules (but Rehnquist probably would have said it was).

What Is the Test of Admissibility?

So this is the basic question before the courts: How do we know whether evidence is testimonial (inadmissible) or not? The answer depends on whether "the primary purpose of the interrogation is to establish or prove past events potentially relevant to later criminal prosecution."

Now let me see if I have this straight. The definition depends on the police officers' purpose when they took a statement. But, as Justice Clarence Thomas noted in his dissent, the Court has repeatedly rejected police purpose in other cases as being "indeterminable and often mixed." Thomas would distinguish between "formal" and "informal" statements. He would consider a Mirandized statement formal (testimonial and inadmissible) but would find the statements in both *Davis* and *Hammon* informal and admissible.

This rationale seems closer to historical intent and easier to apply. But it has a serious flaw: Any test that allows an un-cross-examined 911 call as evidence to convict is simply wrong.

It remains unclear to what extent such calls will be admissible. The majority opinion said that if a 911 operator's purpose shifts from "an interrogation to determine the need for emergency assistance" to "questions designed solely to elicit testimonial evidence from a suspect," then statements made during the call become inadmissible. Good luck to any trial courts trying to determine when that point is reached.

As with 911 interchanges, police questioning of victims and witnesses at the scene of a crime will likely have several functions: finding out what the emergency is and what needs to be done now, as well as discovering generally what happened and gathering evidence to use in court. At one point in its decision, the Court said that only "interrogations solely directed at establishing the facts of a past crime" produce testimonial statements. If so, most statements will be admissible, since police purpose is usually mixed.

But at another point in the opinion, the officer's primary purpose seems to be the test. And *Davis* itself excludes responses to police questioning at the scene.

Take, for example, "Describe the man who hit you," requested at the crime scene or during a 911 call. In general, once the police have arrived, the emergency is over. The same is true if a suspect flees before the victim can call 911. In these situations, the investigators' questions seem designed to elicit testimonial (non-admissible) answers. But when testifying in court, police officers can argue that they needed to get information in order to find and arrest a dangerous, often armed, person, which renders the answer non-testimonial—because it is designed to dispel an ongoing emergency—and admissible.

Cross-Examination Should Be Used When Necessary

Finally, what does all of this have to do with the Sixth Amendment? As a practical matter, the right to confrontation cannot be absolute. As the Court conceded in *Crawford*, certain exceptions to the clause (such as business or government records) have always been recognized? But that's because such records are likely to be reliable and cross-examination would not help. And although it is imprecise and requires a case-by-case analysis, that consideration should be the test.

Forget about "traditional hearsay exceptions." They rarely make sense. The trial judge should simply ask whether or not cross-examination would be useful. If the declarant had reason to lie, was drunk, or was upset, then the statement should not be admitted unless the person who made it can show up to be cross-examined.

Eyewitness statements should never be considered non-testimonial, because cross-examination is always useful to the defense. The testimonial/non-testimonial confusion created by *Crawford* and reinforced in *Davis/Hammon* only takes courts further away from this common-sense approach to confrontation.

But as long as we must abide by the Court's testimonial/non-testimonial dichotomy, there is another way of reading the *Davis/Hammon* decision—one that does not depend on the elusive concept of police purpose. The Court drew a distinction between statements that describe events "as they were actually happening" (non-testimonial) and those that describe past events (testimonial). The majority noted that the testimonial statement in *Hammon* was "neither a cry for help nor the provision of information enabling officers to end a threatening situation."

This distinction is clearer. Under this reasoning, it doesn't matter what the police purpose is. Also, the standard could apply to statements given to a third party—for instance, a rape victim's description of the attack to an examining nurse would be testimonial, regardless of the nurse's intent. I suspect that this is where the Court will ultimately settle.

The Supreme Court should be congratulated for moving away from the often irrational "traditional exceptions to hearsay" approach of *Ohio v. Roberts*, but this decision still doesn't get to the heart of what the Confrontation Clause should be about.

> "'Witness' no longer means witness and
> 'testimonial' has become unmoored
> from the concept of testimony at trial."

Out-of-Court Accusations Are Testimony

Josephine Ross

*A Supreme Court majority tried to clarify what testimony means
in their decision for a combined domestic violence case* Davis v.
Washington *and* Hammon v. Indiana. *They determined that
because a 911 call (*Davis*) took place as events were occurring, it
wasn't testimony but a witness account. They determined, however, that a police interview with a victim after the abuse had
taken place (*Hammon*) was testimony because the information
was given to prove that past events had occurred. If someone's
account is considered testimony, he or she must appear in court
under the Constitution's Confrontation Clause. Associate professor and clinical supervisor of the Criminal Justice Clinic at
Howard University School of Law, Josephine Ross maintains that
the Court confused the distinction between witness and testimony instead of clarifying it. These women's reports should have
been considered testimony, she says, since they were substituted
for the presence of a live witness at a court trial.*

Under the new Confrontation Clause jurisprudence [body
of law] announced in *Crawford [v. Washington]*, asking
whether a statement is testimonial is the same thing as asking
whether an absent witness constitutes a witness for the pur-

poses of the Confrontation Clause [a person's right to be confronted by his accuser]. This Article applauds the Court's connection between the concepts of "witness" and "testimony" and recommends that the connection be strengthened by looking at what these two terms mean in the context of a criminal trial.

When the Supreme Court granted certiorari [allowing a superior court to call on the records of an inferior court] for the cases of *Davis v. Washington* and *Hammon v. Indiana*, the Court had an opportunity to clarify *Crawford* and to reaffirm *Crawford's* goal of live witnesses at trial. Instead, the Court's decision in *Davis/Hammon* created new uncertainties and continued *Crawford's* contradiction between its stated goal for more confrontation and its analysis that shrinks the scope of the Confrontation Clause. Moreover, *Crawford's* central contradiction was no longer just dicta [statement that forms a judgment of the court]. The Court in *Davis/Hammon* determined that whether accusatory statements fell within the Confrontation Clause depended on how the inculpating [incriminating] statements were gathered by the government, rather than whether the statements served the place of live testimony at trial, thereby cementing *Crawford's* contradiction.

The real witness in a trial is not the person who repeats the statement, such as the police officer in *Hammon* or the operator or tape recorder in *Davis*, but the person who made the statement accusing the defendant of a crime. It is the declarant's [person who makes a statement in a legal proceeding] credibility that matters when the fact-finders deliberate about the truth of the charges. Those accusations are "testimonial," for they constitute out-of-court statements that substitute for live testimony at trial. The original purpose of the Confrontation Clause was not to tell the government how to investigate cases but to allow criminal defendants to test the reliability of all testamentary evidence through direct and cross-examination. The Court can recognize this fundamental purpose of the clause without returning to *Roberts* and without turning its back on *Crawford's* promise or its holding. In fact, this recognition is essential to fulfill *Crawford's* promise.

The *Davis/Hammon* decision suffers in its reasoning and clarity because it did not take a functional approach to the evidence before it. The Court flounders around, grabbing different tests as it attempts to differentiate the "testimonial" statements introduced in the *Hammon* trial from the "nontestimonial" statements introduced in the *Davis* trial. In trying to find a principled way to distinguish the statements in *Davis* from *Crawford*, the Court used the state of mind of the witness at the time she made the statement, the immediacy of the crime, and the formality of questioning by the police in addition to analyzing the objective intent of the officer. The Court appears dissatisfied with any particular test to determine testimonial, and fails to provide a clear definition of core testimonial statements in *Davis/Hammon*.

Lower Courts Are Left in Confusion

While the multitude of tests hides some of the incongruities of any one test, it fails to provide true guidance for lower courts applying this new Confrontation Clause jurisprudence. Worse, the confused analysis allows future courts too much leeway in differentiating the statements before them from statements deemed testimonial in *Crawford and Hammon*, thereby encouraging judges to allow in substitutes for live testimony in future trials. Whenever statements fall outside the scope of the newly constituted Confrontation Clause, judges are free to make the same old reliability determinations and decide that having a live witness adds nothing to a jury's ability to render an assessment of the truth of the charge. Hence, the Court needs to be very particular about what type of evidence it excludes from the scope of the clause. With the *Davis/Hammon* case, the Court has arguably created a system in which judges decide the reliability of all accusations except those made in response to government officials whose primary purpose was to establish past events. The prosecutor in *Davis* used the term testimony in the correct sense when she informed the jury that the alleged victim "left you her testimony."

As long as the Court casts its sights backwards, trying to divine the primary purpose that a reasonable officer would have in asking questions or divining the thought process of a reasonable absent witness in making statements, the Court will create a disconnect between the term "witness" as it appears in the Sixth Amendment and the term "witness" as it is commonly understood at trial, meaning a person whose credibility is at issue to the outcome of the charge. After *Crawford and Davis/Hammon*, "witness" no longer means witness and "testimonial" has become unmoored from the concept of testimony at trial.

> "Amy Hammon's subsequent statement
> as to her husband's destruction of their
> property and assault of her were con-
> sistent with the physical evidence . . .
> something was, in fact, wrong."

Courts Must Protect Victims and Not Victimizers

Sarah M. Buel

In the combined domestic violence cases of Davis v. Washington *and* Hammon v. Indiana, *the Supreme Court's majority focused on whether a 911 call (*Davis*) and a police interview (*Hammon*) constituted testimony. If these women's accounts of abuse were considered testimony, rather than just an eyewitness report of events, both women would have had to appear in court so as not to violate their husbands' constitutional right to be confronted by their accusers. Sarah Buel, clinical professor at the University of Texas School of Law and domestic abuse survivor, insists that the majority decision to label the police interview in* Hammon *testimony unfairly protected the rights of the abusive husband instead of the victimized wife. Many women, she says, are too intimidated by their abusers to appear in court. They need their initial accounts of violence to be admissible as evidence whether or not they are present for cross-examination.*

The version of the viewpoint is an excerpt of the original version published in Texas Law Review.

Sarah M. Buel, "*Davis* and *Hammon*: Missed Cues Result in Unrealistic Dichotomy," *Texas Law Review*, vol. 85, no. 2, 2007, pp. 5–7. www.texaslrev.com. Reproduced by permission. The version published herein is an excerpt of the original version published in *Texas Law Review*.

The *Davis* decision reflects a number of false assumptions about the dynamics of domestic violence and how law enforcement should respond to it. Justice [Antonin] Scalia assumes that once an assault has ended, the victim and police officers no longer face danger. The Indiana trial and appellate courts, as well as dissenting Justice [Clarence] Thomas, noted many indications of ongoing danger in *Hammon*. The undisputed facts are that in the dead of winter and in the middle of the night, an obviously traumatized Amy Hammon met law enforcement officers responding to her call for help. Specifically, she was sitting outside on her front porch in Peru, Indiana, a small community in the northern part of the state, on February 26, 2003, at 10:55 PM when the police arrived. She eagerly told the officers "nothing [is] the matter," presumably because her husband, who was already on probation, had dispatched her to get rid of the police before they could enter the home and see the destruction he had wrought.

Concerned for Amy's safety due to her frightened appearance, the officers obtained permission to enter the home and saw gas flames leaping from a stove and shards of shattered glass strewn about the floor. Amy then admitted that her husband had smashed the heater, a phone, and at least one lamp prior to pushing her to the floor, shoving her head into the broken glass, and punching her twice in the chest. The officer testified that after Hershel Hammon repeatedly attempted to interrupt Amy's conversation with the police, Hershel "became angry when I insisted that [he] stay separated from Mrs. Hammon so that we [could] investigate what happened." Certainly, when faced with an increasingly belligerent offender at a domestic violence crime scene, officers are likely to focus on potential danger to themselves and the victim. Given that a substantial number of officers are injured while responding to domestic violence calls, officers who refrain from comprehensive questioning do so at their own peril.

I find it interesting that Justice Scalia cites Amy Hammon's initial statement that nothing was wrong as if it were more reliable than all physical evidence to the contrary. In fact, Amy Hammon's subsequent statement as to her husband's destruction of their property and assault of her were consistent with the physical evidence that something was, in fact, wrong—a house in complete disarray. Yet the majority ignored this critical information. Justice Scalia's apparent suggestion that officers and judges disregard compelling physical evidence in favor of victim statements that were very likely made under duress calls to mind the Richard Pryor [comedian] routine in which he advised adulterous husbands caught in the act to deny wrongdoing and ask their wives, "Are you going to believe me or your lying eyes?"

Perhaps it would have been helpful for Justice Scalia to consult the International Association of Chiefs of Police 1998 Training Manual, *Protecting Victims of Domestic Violence: A Law Enforcement Officer's Guide to Enforcing Orders of Protection Nationwide.* Under the heading of "What Enforcement Action Should be Taken," it instructs police to:

> Ensure the safety of all involved[;] Seek medical attention, if necessary[;] Safeguard the victim from further abuse[;] Secure and protect the crime scene[;] Seek voluntary surrender of firearms for safekeeping purposes[;] Seize firearms subject to State, territorial, local, or tribal prohibitions[;] Identify whether an order of protection has been violated[;] Evaluate the validity and enforceability of the order[;] Arrest for violation of the order where required by the enforcing jurisdiction[;] Arrest for any other criminal offenses[;] Seek an arrest warrant, when required, related to the criminal conduct if the abuser is not at the scene[; and] Attempt to locate and arrest the abuser.

Justice Scalia could also have consulted the Web site of the Columbus, Indiana, police department, which states:

The primary objective in responding to domestic violence calls is to de-escalate violent situations, to protect victims, to reduce officer injury, to reduce repeat calls, to enforce the law against violators, to effect community safety, and to facilitate prosecution, where applicable. The purpose of responding to these calls is also to protect the victim and summon emergency medical care if needed, and to further protect the victim by informing her/him of community resources available such as shelter facilities and support programs.

These police training materials reflect a primary focus on safety, in part because violence most commonly manifests in a community as domestic abuse. According to the National Institute of Justice, 55 percent of American women will be raped or beaten in their lifetimes and 76 percent of the perpetrators of these crimes will be intimate partners. And those are just the crimes reported to police—the Bureau of Justice Statistics found that the police were not notified in half of all intimate partner victimizations. Judges have noted that courts can provide life-saving remedies to victims of domestic violence but are sometimes unaware of the impact of domestic violence on the cases before them. The U.S. Supreme Court should set an example for lower courts, either by correcting the application of the law or by crafting new, more equitable jurisprudence [body of law]. This role is especially important in the *Davis* context because abuse victims are increasingly turning to the courts for help, too often with poor results. Given that the recidivism [repeat offense] rate among domestic violence offenders is two-and-one-half times that of those who assault strangers, there is much room for improvement.

The Statements of Victims Should Be Admitted in Court

Professor [of Constitutional Law at Harvard] Richard Fallon argues that absent fair implementation of constitutional mandates, legal doctrine loses its purpose. The Sixth Amendment right to confrontation must thus be balanced with the need to hold known perpetrators responsible for their crimes. Given that witness intimidation occurs in the majority of domestic violence cases, it must be addressed in Sixth Amendment Confrontation Clause jurisprudence. Violent crime victims are forced to work within a criminal justice system that does not guarantee them a lawyer, due process, privacy, information regarding their cases, consultation with prosecutor, access to court records, or an opportunity to be heard. Although all of the foregoing rights are granted to the accused, none is uniformly granted to crime victims. This disparity reflects the victim's role as a witness in the state's case against the accused and presumes that the prosecutor will protect victims while making optimal use of them to obtain a conviction. However, because domestic violence perpetrators often make it too dangerous for their victims to testify in person, courts should admit victim statements that qualify as hearsay exceptions under a broad definition of testimonial. The most effective jurisprudence is reality-based and can be implemented fairly. Although *Davis* fails on both counts ... judges can do much to ameliorate [soften] its deficiencies by more accurately contextualizing victim statements.

CHAPTER 4

Prosecuting Domestic Abuse Cases Where No Marriage Exists

Case Overview

The State of Ohio v. Michael Carswell (2007)

When Ohio voters passed the state's marriage amendment, they simply wanted to ensure that homosexuals could not legally marry. The average person would have had no idea the legislation would be used to protect those guilty of domestic violence, but that is just what occurred. The amendment defined marriage as a legal agreement between one man and one woman. Michael Carswell and his attorney appealed a lower-court ruling that had found Carswell guilty of violating the state's domestic violence statute by abusing his girlfriend. They filed the appeal on the grounds that because she was not his wife, she deserved no legal recognition according to the marriage amendment. Though the statute protected those people "living as a spouse" as Carswell was with his girlfriend, the marriage amendment did not recognize any such relationship. Essentially, the Supreme Court of Ohio had to determine if the state's domestic violence statute, in recognizing relationships such as Carswell's, nullified the marriage amendment. The court's majority ruled that, because the domestic violence statute did not grant any of the special rights or privileges associated with marriage to those people in a relationship where they were living as a spouse, the statue did not nullify the marriage amendment.

The court's decision brought mixed reviews. Homosexual advocacy groups around the country applauded it. They had expressed concern that if the court found in favor of Carswell, the decision would be used in any state with a similar marriage amendment to deny legal protection to homosexuals abused by their partners with whom they "live as a spouse". On the contrary, Citizens for Community Values, the advocacy group that had campaigned for the marriage amendment, lamented the decision, saying that it had seriously weakened the marriage amendment. They maintained that Ohio's domestic violence statute is flawed. They said that if its language were changed to indicate that everyone living in a household should be protected from violence within it, there would be no legal loophole that could be used to accord the same rights and privileges granted to those living in a legal marriage between one man and one woman to those living in a relationship that only approximated such a marriage. The group insisted that, in crafting the marriage amendment, they had no intention of denying protection or recourse to people abused in an intimate relationship.

> "[The domestic violence statute] does not create any special or additional rights, privileges, or benefits for family or household members."

The State Court's Decision: Unmarried Partners Are Still Responsible for Their Actions

C.J. Moyer

Under Ohio's domestic violence statute, Michael Carswell was convicted of abusing his live-in girlfriend. Carswell's defense team appealed the conviction based on the fact that Ohio has a marriage amendment banning legal recognition of any union involving anyone other than one man and one woman. In State v. Carswell, *the Ohio Supreme Court had to determine whether the statute undermined the marriage amendment by legally recognizing that, though unmarried, Carswell and his girlfriend had a relationship. A majority of justices rejected Carswell's appeal. The following opinion, written by C.J. Moyer, states that because the statute does not grant any rights and privileges of marriage but merely protects a person from another with whom he or she is "living as a spouse," it does not conflict with the marriage amendment.*

In determining whether a statute and a constitutional provision are clearly incompatible, we use the plain and ordinary meaning of the words in question and attempt to reconcile the words of the statute with the terms of the constitution whenever possible. . . .

C.J. Moyer, "The Court's Opinion," in *State v. Carswell*, 114 Ohio St.3d210, 2007-Ohio-3723, December, 2006.

We consider first the terms of the constitutional provision. The first sentence of Section 11, Article XV, prohibits the state from recognizing as a marriage any union between persons other than one man and one woman. That constitutional prohibition is clear and is not at issue in this case. At issue is the second sentence of Section 11, Article XV, which bars the state from creating or recognizing a legal status for unmarried persons that "intends to approximate the design, qualities, significance or effect of marriage." This appeal requires this court to determine whether the indictment of Carswell for knowingly causing or attempting to cause physical harm to a "person living as a spouse" with him is vitiated [invalidated] because the statute under which he was indicted conflicts with the provision of Section 11, Article XV that prohibits the state from creating or recognizing a legal status for unmarried persons that approximates marriage.

The term "legal status" is not defined in the amendment, nor is it defined in the case law of this court. A dictionary definition of the term "status" is succinctly stated as "[a] person's legal condition, whether personal or proprietary; the sum total of a person's legal rights, duties, liabilities, and other legal relations." . . .

The Amendment Was Designed to Protect Heterosexual Marriage

Under these definitions, being married is a status. Marriage gives individuals a standing before the law. Being married gives a person certain legal rights, duties, and liabilities. For example, a married person may not testify against his or her spouse in some situations. . . . A married person may inherit property from a spouse who dies intestate [without a will]. . . . The definition of "status," our understanding of the legal responsibilities of marriage, and the rights and duties created by the status of being married, combined with the first sentence of the amendment's prohibition against recognizing any union that is between persons other than one man and one woman, causes us to conclude that the second sentence of the amendment means that the state cannot create or recognize a legal status for unmarried persons that bears all of the attributes of marriage—a marriage substitute.

When we construe constitutional provisions, "the intent of the framers is controlling. If the meaning of a provision cannot be ascertained by its plain language, a court may look to the purpose of the provision to determine its meaning." . . .

It is clear that the purpose of Issue 1 was to prevent the state, either through legislative, executive, or judicial action, from creating or recognizing a legal status deemed to be the equivalent of a marriage of a man and a woman. The first sentence of the amendment prohibits the recognition of marriage between persons other than one man and one woman. The second sentence of the amendment prohibits the state and its political subdivisions from circumventing the mandate of the first sentence by recognizing a legal status similar to marriage (for example, a civil union).

We next consider whether the prohibitions in Section 11, Article XV, prohibit the state from prosecuting an alleged violation of R.C. 2919.25 when an element to be proved is that the accused is "living as a spouse" with the alleged victim. R.C.2919.25 states:

"(A) No person shall knowingly cause or attempt to cause physical harm to a family or household member.

"(B) No person shall recklessly cause serious physical harm to a family or household member.

"(C) No person, by threat of force, shall knowingly cause a family or household member to believe that the offender will cause imminent physical harm to the family or household member.

"(D)(1) Whoever violates this section is guilty of domestic violence."

R.C. 2919.25(F) defines the term "family or household member":

"(1) 'Family or household member' means any of the following:

"(a) Any of the following who is residing or has resided with the offender:

"(i) A spouse, a person living as a spouse, or a former spouse of the offender;

"(ii) A parent or a child of the offender, or another person related by consanguinity or affinity to the offender;

"(iii) A parent or a child of a spouse, person living as a spouse, or former spouse of the offender, or another person related by consanguinity or affinity to a spouse, person living as a spouse, or former spouse of the offender.

"(b) The natural parent of any child of whom the offender is the other natural parent or is the putative other natural parent.

"(2) 'Person living as a spouse' means a person who is living or has lived with the offender in a common law marital relationship, who otherwise is cohabiting with the offender, or who otherwise has cohabited with the offender within five years prior to the date of the alleged commission of the act in question."

Domestic Violence Defined

The statute distinguishes domestic violence from assault. The conduct of the accused is the same in both instances. Both crimes prohibit the act of "knowingly caus[ing] or attempt[ing] to cause physical harm," but the accused's relationship with the victim is the determining element. Physical harm caused to *another* is an assault, R.C. 2903.13; physical harm caused to a *family or household member* is domestic violence, R.C. 2919.25.

"'The General Assembly enacted the domestic violence statutes specifically to criminalize those activities commonly known as domestic violence. . . .

"In contrast to 'stranger' violence, domestic violence arises out of the *relationship* between the perpetrator and the victim." . . .

The distinction between the two offenses is important because of the large class of potential victims created by R.C. 2919.25(F). The General Assembly clearly intended to offer protections to a wide class of persons. In addition to the contested classification of a "person living as a spouse," the statute recognizes at least eleven other classifications of specific victims: spouse, former spouse, a parent, a child, a blood relative (consanguinity), an in-law (affinity), the parent of a spouse or former spouse, the child of a spouse or former spouse, a blood relative or in-law of a spouse or former spouse, and the natural parent of a child who is also the issue of the offender. . . .

R.C. 2919.25 does not create any special or additional rights, privileges, or benefits for family or household members. Any legal benefits that these persons might possess (such as a right to inherit property through intestacy) are derived from other statutory provisions, not from the person's status as a family or household member in the domestic-violence statute. Additionally, each subset of potential victims has different rights or duties in other statutory provisions. For example, spouses have many other rights and duties, while former spouses do not. By the plain language of the statute, R.C. 2919.25 creates a subset of victims, separate from the generic term "another" in the assault statute; it does not bestow additional rights, duties, or liabilities.

The specific statutory category that Carswell argues violates the constitution is the "person living as a spouse" category. The statute says that "person living as a spouse" means "a person who is . . . cohabiting with the offender, or who . . . has cohabited with the offender within five years" of the alleged crime.

The statute does not define "cohabitation," but we have construed the term in this statute as follows: "The essential elements of 'cohabitation' are (1) sharing of familial or financial responsibilities and (2) consortium." . . . We further explained, "Factors that might establish consortium include mutual respect, fidelity, affection, society, cooperation, solace, comfort, aid of each other, friendship, and conjugal relations." . . . The state does not create cohabitation; rather it is a person's determination to share some measure of life's responsibilities with another that creates cohabitation. The state does not have a role in creating cohabitation, but it does have a role in creating a marriage. . . . The state played no role in creating Carswell's relationship with the alleged victim. Carswell created that relationship.

While the intent of the domestic-violence statute is to protect persons from violence by close family members or residents of the same household, the intent of the marriage amendment was to prevent the creation or recognition of a legal status that approximates marriage through judicial, legislative, or executive action. The statute and the constitution are not in conflict.

We hold, therefore, that the term "person living as a spouse" as defined in R.C. 2919.25 merely identifies a particular class of persons for the purposes of the domestic-violence statutes. It does not create or recognize a legal relationship that approximates the designs, qualities, or significance of marriage as prohibited by Section 11, Article XV of the Ohio Constitution. Persons who satisfy the "living as a spouse" category are not provided any of the rights, benefits, or duties of marriage. A "person living as a spouse" is simply a classification with significance to only domestic-violence statutes. Thus,

R.C. 2919.25 is not unconstitutional and does not create a quasi-marital relationship in violation of Section 11, Article XV of the Ohio Constitution.

> "Using the term 'living as a spouse' within the definition of 'family or household member' clearly expresses an intent to give an unmarried relationship a legal status."

Dissenting Opinion: The Domestic Violence Statute Does Grant Special Rights

J. Lanziger

In State v. Carswell, *a majority of Ohio Supreme Court justices ruled that the state's domestic violence statute did not undermine the state marriage amendment. One judge, J. Lanziger, disagreed. In the following opinion, he maintains that by finding Michael Carswell guilty of domestic violence for beating a woman with whom he was only "living as a spouse," the court was granting marriage rights and privileges to a woman in a relationship that lies outside the amendment's legal definition of marriage between one man and one woman in a recognized and binding marriage contract.*

The disputed portion of Section 11, Article XV, is the second sentence, which says: "This state and its political subdivisions shall not create or recognize a legal status for relationships of unmarried individuals that intends to approximate the design, qualities, significance or effect of marriage." I believe that this language implicitly repeals the domestic violence statute insofar as it applies to "person[s] living as . . . spouse[s]."

J. Lanziger, "Dissenting Opinion," in *State v. Carswell*, 114 Ohio St.3d210, 2007-Ohio-3723, December 2006.

The Majority's Ruling Does Grant "Special Rights"

In discussing Section 11, Article XV's effect on the domestic violence statute and attempting to reconcile the two, the majority first considers the meaning of the term "legal status" as used in the amendment. As the majority points out, the term "status" can be defined expansively as "'[a] person's legal condition, whether personal or proprietary; the sum total of a person's legal rights, duties, liabilities and other legal relations'". . . . The majority appears to accept the . . . definition [which] states that "being married is a status . . . [because it] gives a person certain legal rights, duties; and liabilities," and then concludes that the second sentence of Section 11, Article XV, means that "the state cannot create or recognize a legal status for unmarried persons *that bears all of the attributes of marriage*—a marriage substitute." . . .

Nevertheless, this is not what the disputed sentence says. The legal status prohibited is a legal status "that intends to approximate" *any one* of four attributes—"the design, qualities, significance *or* effect" of marriage. . . . The series is disjunctive [creates on opposition], not conjunctive [connects].

Presumably, under the majority's reasoning, being unmarried does not give one a legal status. Yet unmarried persons living as spouses are covered by the domestic violence statute; they do attain a legal status, albeit a limited one, for each has standing under law to prosecute the other person for an act of domestic violence. If individuals are unmarried and are roommates, for example, they do not have this statutory status. R.C. 2919.25(A) states that "[n]o person shall knowingly cause or attempt to cause physical harm to a family or household member," and "family or household member" includes "[a] spouse, a person living as a spouse, or a former spouse of the offender." "Person living as a spouse" is defined in R.C. 2919.25(F)(2) as "a person who is living or has lived with the offender in a common law marital relationship, who otherwise is cohabiting with the offender, or who otherwise has cohabited with the offender within five years prior to the date of the alleged commission of the act in question."

As noted in Judge Karpinski's dissenting opinion in *State v. Douglas*, ... "[w]hen two unmarried people share financial responsibilities and engage in consortium with one another, what else have we done historically as a society other than to recognize that relationship as one that possesses the 'design, qualities, significance or effect of marriage.'"

Including "person living as a spouse" within the definition of "family or household member" classifies persons who fall into that category as potential domestic violence victims, allowing them additional rights beyond those that would accrue if they were assault victims only. The domestic violence statute is linked to R.C. 2935.03(B)(1) (providing for immediate arrest of the accused) and R.C. 3113.31 (allowing a stronger protection order for the victim). The crime of domestic violence occurs within an intimate relationship and is distinct from the crime of assault.

An assault, a first-degree misdemeanor, is committed when a person "knowingly cause[s] or attempt[s] to cause physical harm to another." ... An initial domestic violence offense is a first-degree misdemeanor but is elevated to a felony on a second offense. . . .

"Living as Spouse" Recognizes a Marriage Relationship

Using the term "living as a spouse" within the definition of "family or household member" clearly expresses an intent to give an unmarried relationship a legal status that approximates the "effect of marriage." The constitutional problem in this case does not arise because cohabiting unmarried persons are included as one of the several groups to whom the domestic violence statutes apply. Instead, the problem is definitional: by using the term "living as a spouse" to identify persons whom the statutes protect and against whom prosecution may be instituted, the General Assembly inherently equates cohabitating unmarried persons with those who are married and extends the domestic violence statutes to persons because their relationship approximates the significance or effect of marriage.

In this case, the statute is challenged solely as it applies to persons living as spouses. Carswell was indicted for knowingly causing or attempting to cause physical harm to a "person living as a spouse" with him. Because R.C. 2919.25 is a criminal statute, it must be strictly construed against the state. . . . Even though I would strike this classification as unconstitutional, as did the trial court, Carswell would still face charges of assault. . . .

It appears that an unintended consequence of the second sentence of Section 11, Article XV, is that the state cannot include unmarried relationships within a statute's protection if in so classifying and defining their status it intends to approximate any one of four attributes of marriage (design, qualities, significance, or effect). In an attempt to reach a more palatable result, the majority concludes that "[w]hile the intent of the domestic-violence statute is to protect persons from violence by close family members or residents of the same household, the intent of the marriage amendment was to prevent the creation or recognition of a legal status *that approximates marriage* through judicial, legislative, or executive action." . . . As attractive as this result is, I cannot agree that the constitution and statute do not conflict. . . .

I respectfully dissent and would reverse the court of appeals and reinstate the trial court's order amending the charge to one of assault.

"Traditional morality alone is a constitutionally inadequate basis for differentiating between married and unmarried perpetrators—and victims—of domestic abuse."

The Ohio Supreme Court Nullified the State Marriage Amendment

Marc Spindelman

According to Marc Spindelman, an associate professor of law at Ohio State University, Ohio's marriage amendment, which was designed to prevent anything but heterosexual marriage, will have unintended consequences. State v. Carswell *called upon Ohio's Supreme Court to rule whether a man who was not married to his girlfriend could still be charged with domestic violence under the state's domestic-violence statute. Spindelman points out that domestic-violence statutes have had to be broadened beyond simple "wife-beating" to include abuse of those "living as a spouse." Such changes have protected a broader range of victims. Refusing to acknowledge that such non-marital and yet nonetheless intimate relationships exist, Spindelman says, is folly, especially in the case of domestic violence.*

They may not realize it yet, but cultural conservatives got some bad news in Ohio. Late in April the state Supreme Court agreed to hear *Ohio v. Carswell*, a case that asks whether the state's recent Marriage Amendment nullifies the legal protections currently afforded unmarried victims of domestic abuse.

Virtually no matter the court's answer, cultural conservatives will lose, setting back efforts in Ohio and elsewhere to pass and enforce anti-gay-marriage amendments, as well as the broader national project of which they're a part—the push to make the law an annex of traditional morality. . . .

She's Not My Wife

Although the Marriage Amendment was sold publicly as a defense against the fearsome hypothetical "threat" of same-sex couples gaily married, *Carswell* actually involves old-school, male-on-female domestic abuse. Michael Carswell was indicted in February 2005 on one count of domestic violence against Shannon Hitchcock, his live-in girlfriend. According to a bill of particulars, he pushed Hitchcock's head down "by her neck, facing [her] to the floor causing injury to her neck, head, and leg." In light of his two prior convictions for domestic abuse, Carswell was charged with a third-degree felony.

In court papers seeking to have the proceedings dismissed, Carswell staked out what was then a relatively novel legal proposition: The Marriage Amendment, he maintained, enjoined [prevented] the state from prosecuting him for domestically abusing Hitchcock, with whom he was, according to the domestic-violence law's provisions, "living as a spouse." The trial court credited his position, amending the charge to one of assault, but was reversed by a unanimous appellate panel. Carswell turned to the state Supreme Court.

To understand Carswell's basic argument, it's useful to put both the state's Marriage Amendment and its domestic-violence law in some context.

The Ohio Marriage Amendment is a sweeping piece of morals legislation. By design, it's an effort to leverage homophobia—in the form of the anti-gay sentiment roused by the Massachusetts Supreme Judicial Court's decision to recognize a constitutional right to same-sex marriage—in order to brand the Ohio Constitution with the broad imprint of traditional moral values.

The amendment begins with a traditional definition of marriage as the exclusive union of one man and one woman. But it then goes far, far beyond that to declare that no intimate relationship other than a traditional marriage shall be created or recognized as a relationship under law: "This state and its political subdivisions shall not create or recognize a legal status for relationships of unmarried individuals that intends to approximate the design, qualities, significance or effect of marriage." . . .

Interestingly, domestic-violence laws, including Ohio's, follow a similar conceptual trajectory from marriage to other relationships. These laws attack what used to be called simply wife beating, a practice that was once, not so very long ago, sanctioned under law as part of the right (and duty) of husbands to chastise their wives. Although wife beating was and is the classic image of domestic violence, it proved to be but one part of a much broader pattern of abuse that women suffered at the hands of men in intimate relationships. Written specifically to address these socially ignored (hence accepted) forms of sex-based violence, domestic-violence laws were typically not limited to wife beating, but encompassed kindred forms of intimate-partner abuse. Eventually, in a number of jurisdictions, Ohio among them, protections against domestic violence were extended to women and men in same-sex relationships—again, based on a wife-beating, hence marriage, model.

Bringing these two strands together, Carswell's position can be stated this way: The Marriage Amendment, which seeks to preserve the unique legal status of marriage, bars the state from treating unmarried individuals like married individuals. The state's domestic-violence law does just that by extending unmarried individuals legal protections against intimate-partner violence on a marriage model. Therefore, the Marriage Amendment invalidates the domestic-violence law as applied to unmarried couples.

Initial Fears About the Amendment Were Founded

If this argument seems fanciful, many thanks are due to the cultural conservatives who backed the Marriage Amendment. They said, Don't worry.

Phil Burress, president of the Ohio group Citizens for Community Values, ran the Ohio Campaign to Protect Marriage, which spearheaded the drive for an amendment. He pooh-poohed concerns that it would eliminate parts of the domestic-violence law. Even after the amendment passed, he continued to insist that the idea that it would be dangerous for unmarried victims of domestic abuse was "on its face absolutely absurd" and "a lot of hypotheticals."

The defensive posture struck an intuitive chord with listeners: What kind of "community values" initiative would help perpetrators, not victims, of domestic abuse?

An unmistakable answer came in legal papers that Burress' associate David Langdon, credited as the author of the Marriage Amendment, filed for Citizens for Community Values in *Ohio v. McIntosh*. Like *Carswell*, *McIntosh* involved a constitutional challenge to the state's domestic-violence law in the wake of the Marriage Amendment. To the benefit of David McIntosh, the perpetrator in the case, Langdon's amicus brief maintains that the Marriage Amendment invalidates the domestic-violence law because, in giving unmarried partners the same legal protections that spouses as spouses get, it fails to recognize the unique status of the marital relationship.

Summarizing the point, the brief contends, "The problem with the domestic-violence statute is that it creates a category of relationship for unmarried couples living as spouses," a category that cannot be squared with the Marriage Amendment, which "intends that marriage remain unique in being the only state-recognized relationship of its type."

Funny, those "absolutely absurd" hypotheticals don't look so absurd or so hypothetical anymore. (To some of us, they never did.)

By taking this position, conservative supporters of the Marriage Amendment have boxed themselves in. If the Ohio Supreme Court ultimately rejects the claim they've supported, it will set a powerful (and, from their perspective, troubling) precedent: That the Marriage Amendment's terms can, and in some instances should, be watered down.

This bodes ill, for example, for efforts cultural conservatives have instigated in *Brinkman v. Miami University,* a case seeking to overturn that Ohio university's decision to offer some unmarried couples the same domestic-partnership benefits provided for years to full-time faculty and staff who are married. If the *Carswell* court reads the Marriage Amendment narrowly out of a recognition, tacit [unspoken] or not, that state protection against intimate-partner abuse is basic to human well-being, what principled grounds could there be for not doing the same thing where domestic-partnership benefits are concerned? Isn't their central aim—providing health insurance to those who need it—also basic to human well-being?

More specifically, what sense would it make to say that the Marriage Amendment allows the state to expend resources on punishing and incarcerating perpetrators of domestic violence who aren't married to their victims, but that it can't help offset those same unmarried victims' health care costs as part of a domestic-partnership program? Beyond none. No legal system based on the rule of reason could properly support it.

Just Plain Unconstitutional

As bad as it would be for cultural conservatives if the Ohio Supreme Court rejected the claim that the Marriage Amendment invalidated the domestic-violence law as applied to unmarried couples, it would be worse for them if it did not. Accepting that claim, along with its conclusion, compels the declaration—in *Carswell* or some future case—that the Marriage Amendment itself is unconstitutional.

For more than thirty years—at least since the U.S. Supreme Court's decision in *Eisenstadt v. Baird* (1972), freshly reaffirmed by *Lawrence v. Texas* (2003)—it's been settled federal constitutional law that the state cannot legitimately draw distinctions between married and unmarried couples for criminal law purposes—certainly not on traditional morality grounds. But there's no conceivable justification aside from traditional morality for Ohio not to recognize the existence of non-marital intimate relationships as such, including their violent realities, through the domestic-violence law. Traditional morality alone is a constitutionally inadequate basis for differentiating between married and unmarried perpetrators—and victims—of domestic abuse.

Remarkably, of the dozens of state court judges in Ohio who have already heard and decided cases involving a Marriage Amendment attack on the domestic-violence law, only Judge James Celebrezze seems to have fully understood and accepted this point. As he concluded last year in *Phelps v. Johnson*, it's both irrational and unreasonable, hence unconstitutional, to distinguish among cases of domestic abuse based upon the marital status of the perpetrator and the victim. As his *Phelps* opinion puts it: "[T]he differentiation between the protections provide[d] married victims of domestic violence, vis-à-vis unmarried victims, bears no rational relationship to a legitimate state interest, and the classifications drawn [along those lines in the Marriage Amendment] are not reasonable in light of its purpose." Judge Celebrezze didn't cite either *Eisenstadt* or *Lawrence* as authority for this reasoning or its upshot—that the Marriage Amendment violates the U.S. Constitution—but he internalized and recapitulated their shared constitutional vision.

Judge Celebrezze got it exactly right in *Phelps*, and the Ohio Supreme Court should follow his lead. But whichever way the *Carswell* court comes out, it is poised to teach cultural conservatives a lesson the anti-domestic-violence movement has been teaching abusers for years: There's a price to pay for the moral hubris it takes to treat people as pawns in your own game.

> *"The domestic violence law could properly criminalize violence by a person against a cohabiter, if the law were drafted to prohibit harm against a 'household member.'"*

Only Married People Can Be Convicted of Domestic Violence

David Langdon

In the case State v. Carswell, *the Supreme Court of Ohio had to decide whether Michael Carswell could be charged under the state's domestic-violence statute for beating his girlfriend even though such relationships were not recognized by the state's new Marriage Amendment. Organizations such as the Citizens for Community Values had backed the Marriage Amendment because it prohibited homosexual marriage. Though the organization did not condone Carswell's behavior, they filed the following brief to the Supreme Court on his behalf. Their attorney David Langdon maintains that if Carswell were found guilty because according to the domestic-violence statute he was "living as a spouse" with this girlfriend, such a ruling would undermine the Marriage Amendment. Landon says any statutory language that grants rights to those not legally married according to the amendment must be changed.*

The ... [Court of Appeals for Warren County] accentuated its misunderstanding of the meaning of the Marriage Amendment in the manner in which it approached the ap-

David Langdon, "Brief of Amicus Curiae of Citizens for Community Values Urging Reversal in *State of Ohio v. Carswell*," in Supreme Court of Ohio, June 19, 2006.

proximation to marriage of relationships which may not be granted legal status. The court mistakenly offered that, "[e]ven if we construed R.C. 2919.25 [the domestic violence statute] to create or recognize a 'legal status for relationships of unmarried individuals,' the statute would still be constitutional because it does not 'intend to approximate the design, qualities, significance, or effect of marriage.' The language of the *statute* expresses no such intent."

But this is not what the Marriage Amendment prohibits. The text of the amendment calls for a focus on what is intended by the *legal status* for the relationship, not the Statute. In *State v. McKinley*, 2006-Ohio-2507, the Third Appellate District properly interpreted the Marriage Amendment on this point, stating the "*relationship* must intend to approximate marriage, not the statute itself." For the status is inextricably bound up in the purpose of the relationship referenced in the statute. The intention for the appearance of the relationship in a statute as a relationship of legal consequence cannot be divorced from the purpose of the relationship itself, for the statutory recognition countenances the referenced relationship *as it is*. Thus, if the relationship is one intending to approximate marriage in a relevant respect, then so also does the legal status. The legal status simply mirrors the relationship's factual nature in its grant of legal recognition. There is no divide between the two.

Status Must Be Distinguished from Benefits

An additional and significant error in the lower court's presentation was its ignoring the distinction between the status of a relationship, and the benefits which are assigned as a result of membership in that relationship given the status. On page 6 of the court's opinion, the court exemplifies this defining confusion.

> The statute does not permit unmarried individuals to enter into a legally binding, marriage-like relationship with each

other. It does not give an unmarried individual the right to inherit from an intestate cohabitant, the right to make medical decisions on a cohabitant's behalf, the right to file a joint tax return with a cohabitant, or any other of the host of rights associated with marriage.

While all of these assertions may be accurate, they are also irrelevant to the question of whether the statute creates or recognizes a legal status for a relationship that approximates marriage in design, qualities, significance or effect. Clearly, creating a legal status for unmarried couples in marriage-like relationships is a violation of the Constitution. But the "rights and benefits analysis" adds nothing to this conclusion, and it can only mislead. Whichever right, obligation or benefit, the state will subsequently assign (or not) to those in the marriage-approximating relationship is irrelevant. The focus of the second sentence of the Marriage Amendment is not on the benefits or obligations assigned to those in the relationship which is given a legal status—it is on the *status itself*. These two matters (benefits and status) must be assidously [vigorously] distinguished for the amendment to be properly understood.

The Marriage Amendment does *not* proscribe the extension of benefits to persons in marriage-mimicking relationships. Rather, it proscribes *the very legal recognition* of the relationships in the first place, for any purpose. Thus, for instance, if the State were to want to grant medical benefits to all those who "reside with state employees," the Marriage Amendment would extend no prohibition to this—even though many of these benefits-receiving co-residents qualified thereunder may well be in a marriage-mimicking relationship (*e.g.*, domestic partnerships). Because the State (in this hypothetical) would extend this benefit on grounds *other than* the presence of a marriage-approximating relationship, the Marriage Amendment has no application. Conversely, if a legal status were given to a marriage-approximating relationship, with no concomitant grant of a benefit or obligation that is customarily associated with marriage, the status is nonetheless quite clearly prohibited by the Constitution. . . .

The Domestic Violence Law Is Flawed

Accordingly, to bring this idea to the matter herein dispute the domestic-violence law could *properly* criminalize violence by a person against a cohabiter, if the law were drafted to prohibit harm against a "household member" that indeed was defined to include all "members of a household," or all those who reside together. This would certainly encompass those cohabiting, or "living as spouses," as well as dorm-mates, live-in nannies, and the like. But again, the propriety of this extension exists because in such a case no relationship which intends to approximate marriage in relevant respects has been given a legal status by the law; rather a broader, benign category of persons would be protected (which may properly encompass those in relationships which may not be given *independent* legal recognition).

The problem with the domestic-violence statute is that it creates a category of relationship for unmarried couples living as spouses. Had "household members" been more broadly defined (and with more terminological consistency), no constitutional problem would be here presented. This is why the remedy is so simply accomplished. By making this change, the legislature would thereby include in its coverage and extend the penalties against those who act violently toward those who share their home, but who are not "living as spouses," such as roommates. Both of these latter categories of persons are just as susceptible to the particular dangers that are sought to be addressed by the present domestic violence statute, but these persons have been excluded from coverage under the law for undetermined reason. Making this appropriate change to law to embrace all household members rather than simply those now listed in the statute would maintain the present penalties against those who harm those "living as their spouse" (without so designating them), while also extending this treatment to others similarly situated.

Of course, and most relevantly, this would also remove the constitutional defect with the law. The Marriage Amendment does not proscribe the receipt of benefits or obligations by persons in marriage-approximating relationships; it proscribes the government's formal recognition of such relationships in the law. The Marriage Amendment intends that marriage remain unique in being the only state-recognized relationship of its type. While an unlimited number of protections, benefits, or obligations may be extended to all persons in Ohio, regardless of the kind of relationships these persons maintain those protections, benefits or obligations may *not* be extended by the State to them *because of* a person's membership in the marriage-approximating relationship. The State may deal however it wishes with *individuals*; it may *not* recognize a legal status for marriage-approximating *relationships*.

> *"Surely the voters of Ohio did not con-*
> *template that the amendment they*
> *passed would be used to deny a woman*
> *protection from a domestic abuser."*

Many Domestic Violence Laws Conflict with State Marriage Amendments

Joanna Grossman

In the following piece, FindLaw columnist and professor of law at Hofstra University Joanna Grossman lauds the Supreme Court of Ohio for protecting the rights of cohabiting people even if their relationships are not recognized under the state's anti-same-sex marriage amendment. The Court ruled in State v. Carswell *that even though Michael Carswell was only "living as a spouse" with his girlfriend—a relationship not recognized by the Marriage Amendment—he could still be charged for beating her under the state's domestic violence statute. Grossman points out that recognizing the right of people not to be beaten by their live-in boyfriend or girlfriend does not in any way confer upon them the status of marriage with all its other legal privileges.*

Ohio law criminalizes domestic violence, defining the offense as causing or attempting to cause physical harm to a "family or household member." Can one party to a same-sex couple avail himself or herself of this law's protection against the other, on the ground that he or she is a "family or household member"?

Joanna Grossman, "An Ohio Supreme Court Case Interprets the State's Anti-Same-Sex-Marriage Amendment," *How the Court Protected Unmarried, Cohabiting Couples from Domestic Violence Despite the Amendment*, August 7, 2007. http://writ.lp.findlaw.com. Copyright © 1994–2008 FindLaw, a Thomson business. Reproduced by permission.

In *Ohio v. Carswell*, the Ohio Supreme Court answered yes. Its reasoning turned not only on the usual questions of statutory interpretation, but also on its construction of the state's anti-same-sex marriage constitutional amendment.

The Crime of Domestic Violence, as Defined by Ohio Law

Prior to the 1970s, domestic violence had no special place in the law. Prosecutors seeking to charge those who perpetrated abuse against a family member with a crime could only invoke the assault and battery statutes. Yet these laws often did not provide sufficient protection against violence and threats of violence in the home. In addition, police and courts were hesitant to intervene in spousal relationships, so even laws that should have been applied often were not.

Beginning with Pennsylvania in 1976, however, every state adopted a law to make civil protection orders available to victims of domestic violence. Many states also tinkered with police procedures and other policies to make it easier for domestic violence victims to make use of applicable criminal laws. For example, they adopted mandatory arrest laws in such cases to ensure that a victim would not, after the police had departed, be forced to immediately face an abuser who was irate because she'd called the police.

In addition, some states began to separately define a crime of "domestic violence" or "domestic assault"—one element of which was an intimate relationship between perpetrator and victim. The Ohio provision at issue in *Carswell* is just such a law.

Section 2919.25 of the Ohio Code criminalizes "domestic violence," which it defines as the crimes of assault or menacing when directed at a "family or household member." (Assault is defined as knowingly causing or attempting to cause physical harm, or recklessly causing serious physical harm. The offense of menacing is defined as knowingly causing another to fear physical harm.)

A surprisingly large number of state and local laws—in areas ranging from zoning, to housing assistance, to rent control, to wrongful death, to name just a few—make benefits, burdens, or criminal responsibility turn on family or marital status. The applicable statutes often use terms like "household member," "spouse," or "family" without defining them. Thus, courts are left to supply their own definition, and the definition often properly varies along with the purpose of the statute at issue.

Ohio's domestic violence law prohibits harming a "family or household member." The statute goes on to define those terms to include, among others, "a spouse, a person living as a spouse, or a former spouse of the offender."

A person "living as a spouse" is defined, in turn, as someone "who is living or has lived with the offender in a common law marital relationship, who otherwise is cohabiting with the offender, or who otherwise has cohabited with the offender within five years prior to the date of the alleged commission of the act in question."

Can Non-Spouses Be Convicted?

The case before the Ohio Supreme Court arose out of the February 2005 indictment of Michael Carswell, under Section 2919.25, for one count of domestic violence. Carswell was alleged to have choked his live-in girlfriend, and thus plainly his "family or household member" as defined under the Ohio statute.

Carswell filed a motion to dismiss the indictment. He argued that the law, as applied to him, violated Section 11, Article XV of the Ohio Constitution, which provides:

"Only a union between one man and one woman may be a marriage valid in or recognized by this state and its political subdivisions. This state and its political subdivisions shall not create or recognize a legal status for relationships of unmarried individuals that intends to approximate the design, qualities, significance or effect of marriage."

This amendment was adopted by Ohio Voters in the November 2004 elections; similar amendments have been adopted in twenty-six other states. Its purpose was not only to prevent the adopting state from celebrating same-sex marriages, but also to prevent it from recognizing any other states' same-sex marriages as valid. (To date, only Massachusetts has legalized same-sex marriage, but at the time the amendment was passed, some observers anticipated other states' doing the same.)

But these goals were both accomplished by the first sentence of the amendment.

In the second sentence, Ohio's voters went even further, by also prohibiting the state from recognizing any status for unmarried individuals that approximates "the design, qualities, significance or effect of marriage." Plainly, Ohio was targeting civil unions and the like, which give the legal incidents of marriage but withhold the name "marriage" for the union.

Other states have similarly targeted civil unions with their amendments. But Ohio's amendment is unusual in that its broader reach is not limited to same-sex relationships. Rather, by its own terms, it applies to all "unmarried individuals".

Carswell's claim, then, is that Ohio's domestic violence statute violates Section 11, Article XV of the Constitution by, in effect, creating a "legal status" for unmarried couples where the victim lives as a spouse with the offender—but is not actually legally a spouse—and defining "living as a spouse" to include simple cohabitation.

Unmarried Couples Can Have Rights Without Status

In a six-one ruling, the Ohio Supreme Court rejected Carswell's claim.

For the majority, the key issue was what the amendment meant by "legal status," which neither the amendment nor any Ohio precedent had defined. . . .

The majority reasoned as follows: If, by granting domestic violence protection to unmarried couples, the legislature conferred a "legal status" upon them, then the law conflicts with the constitutional ban, and is void. In contrast, if the legislature merely granted such couples a legal right, without a concomitant status, then the domestic violence law can survive constitutional scrutiny.

Marriage itself is the quintessential "legal status," in that the exchange of "I dos" gives rise to a set of legal rights, duties, and liabilities, touching upon areas of law like inheritance, torts, evidence, divorce and property distribution, and so on. And clearly what the Ohio voters intended to accomplish with the amendment was to ban the legislature from creating a marriage-like status for same-sex couples.

Carswell argued that the domestic violence law had done just that, in violation of the amendment, by applying a special assault law to offenders who live "as a spouse" with their victim. However, the argument did not ring true to the majority, for two key reasons:

First, the domestic violence law did not simply equalize cohabiting couples with opposite-sex married couples with respect to domestic violence protection. Instead, it swept in many offender-victim pairs—such as two former spouses, a parent and a child, and co-parents, to name just a few.

Second, cohabitation itself is not typically a legal status. The law creates marriages, by issuing licenses and prescribing rules for solemnization. In contrast, people live together without any help (or hindrance) from the law at all.

The majority thus concluded that the domestic violence law "merely identifies a particular class of persons for the purposes of the domestic violence statutes. It does not create or recognize a legal relationship that approximates the designs, qualities, or significance of marriage as prohibited by the [Ohio constitution.]"

One Justice on the Ohio Supreme Court dissented, arguing that the constitutional amendment prohibits the creation of a legal status that approximates any one of marriage's attributes—its designs, qualities, significance, or effect of marriage. On this view, granting special protection against assault based on the relationship between the offender and victim is one of the "effects" of marriage.

The upshot of the majority's ruling is that Michael Carswell, a repeat offender, now faces up to five years for the assault of his girlfriend. In addition, other domestic violence victims will continue to enjoy the protection of the full, intended scope of the law.

That's good news—but this case should never have gotten this far. (It did so in part because the trial court ruled in favor of Carswell, based on rulings from appellate courts in two prior, similar cases.) Surely the voters of Ohio did not contemplate that the amendment they passed would be used to deny a woman protection from a domestic abuser simply because the couple was not married.

Unintended Consequences

At this point, almost every state in the Union has enacted either a constitutional amendment, statute, or both, designed to prohibit the celebration or recognition of same-sex marriage. But some—like Ohio's—are drafted broadly to ban not only marriage, but any legal recognition of same-sex relationships.

As I have discussed in several previous columns such as this one, these laws are historically unprecedented—particularly to the extent they seek to reach beyond marriage to all forms of legal recognition.

Moreover, these laws are in many cases poorly drafted, and likely to produce unintended consequences—such as the trial court's initial acceptance of Michael Carswell's argument that the amendment prevented his prosecution.

Another example comes from an appellate court in Michigan. In the case of *National Pride at Work v. Governor of Michigan*, that court recently ordered all public universities, state agencies, and local governments to cease providing health insurance to the partners of gay and lesbian employees because of a 2004 constitutional amendment stating that only a union of one man and one woman is valid "as a marriage or . . . for any purpose." A decision to opt to give equal health insurance benefits is very different from the compulsion to do so, and as in the Ohio case, it's unlikely that here, Michigan voters affirmatively intended, by their amendment, to prohibit the government from offering health insurance benefits in a fair and non-discriminatory way.

The intended consequences of such laws—to systematically deny rights to gays and lesbians based solely on animus [bad feelings] against them—are bad enough. Their unintended consequences only pour salt into the wound these amendments create. Voters and legislatures should be cautious lest they discover that they have allowed irrational fear and hostility to menace the integrity of their state codes and constitutions.

Organizations to Contact

The editors have compiled the following list of organizations concerned with the issues debated in this book. The descriptions are derived from materials provided by the organizations. All have publications or information available for interested readers. The list was compiled on the date of publication of the present volume; the information provided here may change. Be aware that many organizations take several weeks or longer to respond to inquiries, so allow as much time as possible.

American Bar Association Commission on Domestic Violence
740 Fifteenth Street NW, Washington, DC   20005-1019
(202) 622-1000
Web site: www.abanet.org

Founded in 1994, the American Bar Association Commission on Domestic Violence helps individual attorneys who defend victims of domestic violence. The commission's resources include research assistance, sample practice tools, model pleadings in domestic violence cases, and access to legal experts in the field of domestic violence defense.

Battered Women's Justice Project
125 S. Ninth Street, Suite 302, Philadelphia, PA   19107
(800) 903-0111, ext. 3
Web site: www.bwjp.org

The Battered Women's Justice Project provides resources for advocates, battered women, legal and justice system personnel, policy makers, and others engaged in the justice system's response to domestic violence. The project also wants to create systemic change within community organizations and governmental agencies to hold these institutions accountable for the goals of safety and security for battered women and their children.

FaithTrust Institute
2400 N. Forty-Fifth Street, #10, Seattle, WA   98103
(206) 634-1903
Web site: www.faithtrustinstitute.org

The FaithTrust Institute is an interfaith organization working to end domestic violence around the world. The institute provides community shelters, attorneys, and advocacy groups with tools to understand the unique cultural roots of domestic violence. Founded in 1977, the FaithTrust Institute works with many communities, including Asian and Pacific Islander, Buddhist, Jewish, Latino, Muslim, Black, Anglo, Indigenous, Protestant, and Roman Catholic.

Family Violence Prevention Fund
383 Rhode Island Street, Suite 304, San Francisco, CA   94103
(415) 252-8900
Web site: www.endabuse.org

Founded in the 1980s, the Family Violence Prevention Fund (FVPF) has developed programs and sponsored initiatives to curb violence against women and children around the world. FVPF was a key player in crafting the landmark Violence Against Women Act passed by Congress in 1994. The FVPF works within local communities to promote leadership among men and youth that will end the cycle of violence. FVPF is also committed to ensuring that violence prevention efforts in the health care and criminal justice environments become self-sustaining.

Human Rights Campaign Fund Federal Advocacy Network
1640 Rhode Island Avenue NW, Washington, DC   20036
(800) 777-4723
Web site: www.hrc.org

The Human Rights Campaign Federal Advocacy Network works to end discriminatory policies against gay, lesbian, bisexual, and transgendered (GLBT) people. Since many states have passed marriage amendments, the network has worked to ensure that such amendments do not deny these individuals legal protection against intimate partner violence.

Lamda Legal Defense and Education Fund
120 Wall Street, Suite 1500, New York, NY 10006
(212) 809-8585
Web site: www.lamdalegal.org

The Lamda Legal Defense and Education Fund provides education and funding to ensure that gay, lesbian, bisexual, and transgendered (GLBT) people are not denied their civil rights. In particular, they provide legal guidance and assistance to GLBT people impacted by domestic violence.

National Domestic Violence Hotline
PO Box 161810, Austin, TX 78716
Hotline: (800) 799-SAFE (7233)
Web site: www.ndvh.org

The National Domestic Violence Hotline is a crisis hotline dedicated to providing uninterrupted, free, and rapid assistance to domestic violence victims across the United States and its territories. The hotline acts as a clearinghouse, connecting individuals to safe and reliable agencies and services in their communities.

National Network to End Domestic Violence
660 Pennsylvania Avenue SE, Suite 303
Washington, DC 2003
(202) 543-5566
Web site: www.nnedv.org

The National Network to End Domestic Violence (NNEDV) is dedicated to affecting real social change by helping create a social, political, and economic environment where domestic violence is a thing of the past. NNEDV acts as a liaison between advocacy groups and care providers and the federal government to ensure that abused women get the understanding, resources, and care they need.

Nursing Network on Violence Against Women, International
PMB 165, Modesto, CA   95354-1215
(888) 909-9993
Web site: www.nnvawi.org

Founded in 1985 during the first National Nursing Conference on Violence Against Women, the Nursing Network on Violence Against Women is a group of nurses that focuses on health issues relating to domestic violence and other sexual and emotional violence against women. In recognition of its growing international membership, the organization recently added International to its name.

For Further Research

Books

Ola Barnett, Cindy L. Miller-Perrin, and Robin Perrin, *Family Violence Across the Lifespan: An Introduction*. Thousand Oaks, CA: Sage Publications, 2004.

Sandra L. Brown, *How to Spot a Dangerous Man*. Alameda, CA: Hunter House, 2005.

Angela Browne, *When Battered Women Kill*. New York: Free Press, 1987.

Carl G. Buzawa and Eve S. Buzawa, *Domestic Violence: The Criminal Justice Response*. Thousand Oaks, CA: Sage Publications, 1996.

Raoul Felder and Barbara Victor, *Getting Away with Murder: Weapons for the War Against Domestic Violence*. New York: Simon & Schuster, 1996.

Pamala Jayne, *Ditch That Jerk! Dealing with Men Who Control and Hurt Women*. Alameda, CA: Hunter House, 2000.

Anne Jones, *Women Who Kill*. New York: Holt, Rinehart and Winston, 1980.

Janine Latus, *If I Am Missing or Dead*. New York: Simon & Schuster, 2006.

L.G. Mills, *Insult to Injury: Rethinking Our Responses to Intimate Abuse*. Princeton, NJ: Princeton University Press, 2003.

Anson Shupe, William A. Stacey, and Lonnie R. Hazelwood, *Violent Men, Violent Couples: the Dynamics of Domestic Violence*. Lexington, MA: Lexington Books, 1987.

Marilee Strong, *Erased: Missing Women, Murdered Wives*. San Francisco, CA: Jossey-Bass, 2008.

Lenore E. Walker, *Terrifying Love: Why Battered Women Kill and How Society Responds*. New York: Harper Perennial, 1989.

Elaine Weiss, *Surviving Domestic Violence: Voices of Women Who Broke Free*. Scottsdale, AZ: Agreka Books, 2000.

K.J. Wilson, *When Violence Begins at Home: A Comprehensive Guide to Understanding and Ending Domestic Abuse*. Alameda, CA: Hunter House, 2006.

General Articles

R. Bachman and D. Carmody, "Fighting Fire with Fire: The Effects of Victim Resistance in Intimate Versus Stranger Perpetrated Assaults Against Females," *Journal of Family Violence*, vol. 9, 1994.

Arnold Binder and James W. Meeker, "Experiments as Reforms," *Journal of Criminal Justice*, vol. 18, 1998.

Dave Breakenridge, "Tools of the Trade: High-Tech Gadgets Give Stalkers More Power," *Winnipeg Sun*, February 8, 2005.

Michelle Chen, "Abuse Survivors Face Systemic Struggles as Resources for Help Dwindle," Women's International Perspective. http://thewip.net.

Franklyn W. Dunford, "The Measurement of Recidivism in Cases of Spousal Assault," *Journal of Criminal Law and Criminology*, vol. 83, 1992.

Sue Else, "How I Would End Violence Against Women," March 28, 2008. www.mylifetime.com.

Jamie Francisco, "Domestic Violence Websites Offer Escape Link," *Chicago Tribune*, August 7, 2006.

Pablo Fernandez, "Men Urged to Speak Out," *The Calgary Sun*, May 11, 2006.

Richard Gelles, "Constraints Against Family Violence: How Well Do They Work," *American Behavioral Scientist*, vol. 36, 1993.

Kris Henning and Lynette Feder, "A Comparison of Men and Women Arrested for Domestic Violence: Who Presents the Greater Threat," *Journal of Family Violence*, April 2004.

Machaela M. Hoctor, "Domestic Violence as a Crime Against the State," *California Law Review*, vol. 85, 1997.

Michael P. Johnson, "Domestic Violence: It's Not About Gender—Or Is It?" *Journal of Marriage and Family*, vol. 67, 2005.

Lauren Knight, "Proposed Cuts to Federal Funds to Impact Local Programs Working to End Violence Against Women," February 11, 2008. www.ksby.com.

Mary P. Koss, "Blame, Shame, and Community: Justice Responses to Violence Against Women," Minnesota Center Against Violence and Abuse, 2000. www.mincava.umn.edu.

————and Truc-Nhu Ho, "Domestic Violence in a Southern City: The Effects of a Mandatory Arrest Policy on Male-Versus-Female Aggravated Assault Incidents," *American Journal of Criminal Justice*, vol. 25, 2000.

C.J. Newton, "Domestic Violence: An Overview," *Mental Health Journal*, February 2001.

Philanthropy Journal, "Escaping Domestic Violence," June 26, 2006.

Janell Schmidt and Lawrence W. Sherman, "Does Arrest Deter Domestic Violence," *American Behavioral Scientist*, vol. 36, 1993.

Lawrence W. Sherman and Richard A. Berk, "The Specific Deterrent Effects of Arrest for Domestic Assault," *American Sociological Review*, vol. 49, 1984.

A. Smith, "Domestic Violence Laws: The Voices of Battered Women," *Violence and Victims*, vol. 16, 2001.

People v. Francine Hughes

Michael Dowd, "The 'Battered Women's Defense': Its History and Future." http://library.findlaw.com.

Joshua Dressler, "Battered Women and Sleeping Abusers: Some Reflections." moritzlaw.osu.edu.

Stanton Peele, "Making Excuses: Betrayed Men and Battered Women Get Away with Murder," *National Review*, November 21, 1994.

Castle Rock v. Gonzales

Alison Bowen, "U.S. Violence Case to Get Human Rights Review," October 26, 2007. www.womensenews.org.

Michelle Chen, "International Suit Filed Against Cops for Ignoring Mom's Pleas," *The New Standard*, January 5, 2006.

Marcia Coyle, "Supreme Court to Weigh In on Due Process and Domestic Violence," *The National Law Journal*, March 9, 2005.

Linda Greenhouse, "Justices to Mull Rights of Those Seeking Police Protection," *New York Times*, November 2, 2004.

Debra Rosenberg, "A Matter of Restraint," *Newsweek*, March 19, 2005.

Davis v. Washington and Hammon v. Indiana

David Feige, "Domestic Silence: The Supreme Court Kills Evidence-Based Prosecution," Slate, March 12, 2004. http://slate.msn.com.

Linda Greenhouse, "Justices Weigh In on Use of Tapes and Transcripts," *New York Times*, March 21, 2006.

———, "911 Call Is Held as Evidence if Victim Cannot Testify," *New York Times*, June 20, 2006.

Nicholas Lancaster, "The Framers' Sixth Amendment Prescriptions: Cross-examination and Counsel of Choice," Judge Advocate General's School, 2007. www.au.af.mil/au/cpd/jagschool/.

Charles Lane, "Absent Accusers' 911 Calls Ruled Admissible," *Washington Post*, June 20, 2006.

Tony Rizzo, "Justices Ponder Use of Evidence: Domestic Abuse Cases Face Crucial Judgment," *Kansas City Star*, March 25, 2006.

David Savage, "Justices May Further Restrict Domestic Violence Testimony," *Los Angeles Times*, March 20, 2006.

State of Ohio v. Carswell

Chris Johnson, "Ohio Supreme Court Decision to Uphold Domestic Violence Law May Also Place Civil Unions Further out of Reach for GLBT Community." www.hrc-backstory.org.

Dahlia Lithwick, "Please Say 'I Don't,'" *Washington Post*, November 5, 2006.

Richard J. Rosendall, "Marriage Aftershocks in Ohio," *Bay Windows*, August 2, 2007.

Marc Spindelman, "The Whipsaws of Backlash," 2007. www.moritzlaw.osu.edu.

Index

Borderline syndrome diagnosis (of Hughes), 25–26

Bowers v. DeVito (1982), 70

Bradley, Craig M., 98–104

Brinkman v. Miami University, 132

Browne, Angela, 46

Buel, Samuel, 109–113

Bureau of Justice Statistics, 45

The Burning Bed movie, 21, 22, 50–51

BWS. See Battered Wife Syndrome (BWS)

C

Carr, Wanda, 32

Carswell, Michael. *See Ohio vs. Michael Carswell*

CCADV. See Colorado Coalition Against Domestic Violence (CCADV)

Celebrezze, James, 133–134

Center for Constitutional Law, 51

Chandler, June, 31

Citizens for Community Values, 115–116, 135

Cohen, Richard, 37–40

Colorado

  arrest statutes, 63–65

  denial of discretionary enforcement, 66

  failure to enforce TRO procedures, 81–82

  General Assembly omnibus legislation, 64

  restraining order enforceability determination, 57–61

  Roll Call Trainings by police, 74–75

  State Supreme Court issues, 62–63

  See also Town of Castle Rock, Colorado v. Gonzales (2005)

Colorado Coalition Against Domestic Violence (CCADV), 74

Confrontation Clause (Sixth Amendment, U.S. Constitution)

  balancing with perpetrator's needs, 112–113

  intentions of, 99–101, 105–107

  lower court confusion about, 98–99, 107–108

  911 call admissibility, 89

  nonabsolute nature of, 103

  testimony requirements of, 87, 91–92, 96

  use in *Ohio v. Roberts,* 99

  vulnerabilities of, 94

  See also Davis v. Washington; Hammon v. Indiana

Constitution (U.S.). *See* Confrontation Clause; Fourteenth Amendment; Sixth Amendment

Courts. *See* Lower courts; Supreme Court

Crawford, Sylvia, 92–94

Crawford v. Washington, testimonial issues, 92–94

Cross-examination, 102–104

D

Davis, Adrian. *See Davis v. Washington* (2006)

Davis v. Washington (2006)

  admissibility reliability test, 101–102

  case overview, 85–86

  Confrontation Clause issues, 87, 89, 91–92, 94, 96–97, 98–100

  911 call response issue, 87–89, 100–101

  nonfunctional approach to evidence, 107

  out-of-court accusations, 105–108